18.95

The Continuity of Salvation

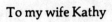

To my wife Kathy

The Continuity
of Salvation

A Study of Paul's Letter
to the Romans

by Theodore M. Snider

McFarland & Company, Inc., Publishers
Jefferson, North Carolina, and London

Library of Congress Cataloging in Publication Data

Snider, Theodore M., 1942–
    The continuity of salvation.

    Bibliography: p.
    Includes index.
    1. Bible. N.T. Romans — Criticism, interpretation,
etc. 2. Jews in the New Testament. I. Title.
BS2665.2.S65 1984   227'.106   84-42602

ISBN 0-89950-126-5

Printed in the United States of America.

McFarland Box 611 Jefferson NC 28640

Table of Contents

Preface

The task of interpreting Paul's letter to the Romans has been undertaken by numerous scholars who have spent a lifetime with the Christian scriptures and traditions. In the pages which follow, I do not wish to discredit or disregard their efforts. Their labors have meant much. However, this study wishes to demonstrate that most of these interpretations have relied on christological traditions at the expense of theological traditions. An adequate understanding of Palestine and Judaism at the beginning of the Common Era has been missing. The religious ferment arising out of the history of the Exile and the intertestamental period has also been missing.

I do not presume to offer a fully developed interpretation of Paul's letter to the Romans. This is a work in progress, one which tries to take into account the beliefs and events surrounding the ministry of Jesus and of Paul.

One presupposition of this work is that "historical objectivity is not a reconstruction of the past in its unrepeatable factuality; it is the truth of the past in the light of the present."[1*] Such factuality would indeed be unrepeatable and thus its reconstruction in pristine form, impossible. In this work we shall try to reconstruct the times as accurately as present research allows.

Lamar Williamson illustrates how difficult it is to unite text and background, and the even greater difficulty of uniting the text with *intended* meaning. He writes about questions raised in Galatians 3:11 and Romans 1:17:

*See Chapter Notes, beginning on page 169.

1

The fact that no two of these translations [KJV, ASV, RSV, NEW, JB, TEV] say exactly the same thing is ample witness to both the importance and the difficulty of the sentence. An additional complication arises from the fact that Paul here quotes directly the Greek translation of Habakkuk 2:4. Thus the interpreter must ask what the Hebrew text intended in its original context, then what interpretive moves may have occurred when it was translated into Greek, then what shifts in meaning may be implied by Paul's use of the sentence in the present context.[2]

Williamson then points out that the RSV, NEB, and TEV understand "faith" in this instance to be prerequisite to and the ground of justification, whereas in the KJV, ASV, and JB "faith" is a means to life or a new quality of life.[3]

This is but one issue with which the interpreter is confronted. The christological/theological problem in Paul surfaces in the translation, "faith *in* Christ Jesus." The Greek word here translated "in" can also mean "of." "In" reflects a christological meaning, whereas "of" points to a theological meaning. It is the contention of this present study that Paul's writing is basically theological.

Legrand points to the problems with translating when he asks, Should translation go back to the oldest "original" meaning of the text, or should it enter into the creativity of language and the dynamic process of on-going reinterpretation of the texts already at work in the Old Testament traditions and redactions?[4] It is the intention of this study to take both into consideration with a primary emphasis on the latter.

In this work we shall demonstrate that the theological meaning is intended by Paul, and that this results in Romans with the central theme of the faithfulness and graciousness of God. When justification by faith is made the central issue, as with the Reformers and most of the Church to this day, Paul is made to appear highly individualistic, anti-Judaic, and the promoter of a new form of legalism. We shall argue in these pages that the theme of God's faithfulness forms a more solid foundation on which to base our response of faith. In this way we can understand in a most radical manner Paul's message that "there is no distinction" between persons or groups of persons. Indeed, this is the radical claim of Paul that the Church in its particularism has for centuries been unable to accept!

Therefore, the work that is here proposed is long overdue. The signs of anti-Judaism are still with us despite the Jewishness that runs like a golden thread through the Church's scriptures and traditions. *The Jewish Declaration* of 1965 (*Nostra Aetate*, No. 4), growing out of the call issued by the Second Vatican Council, has prepared the way for a proper re-Judaizing of Christianity. As Monica Hellwig states the issue: "That means that we who are Christians must learn to think of our identity as that of a sect of Jews who have acquired a huge Gentile membership."[5] Whether that is possible after 1900 years of separateness is questionable. And yet this is a fundamental issue for the Church in our day. This means that the particularism of the Church must be called into question, including the simple time designations of B.C. and A.D. In this study we will use the designations of B.C.E. and C.E.

I wish to acknowledge my indebtedness to the late rabbi Sidney Steiman of Indianapolis whose encouragement in this study was most valuable. To Dr. Clark Williamson and Dr. Calvin Porter, I extend my appreciation for their contagious interest in this subject. And to the dedicated members of the various study groups in which these thoughts were fleshed out, I give my thanks for their bearing with me in some mind-stretching discussion.

Introduction

Paul wrote his letter to the congregations in Rome around 56 C.E. in order to bring about a genuine unity of faith among Jews, Christian Jews, and Gentile Christians. In order to bring this about, Paul emphasized the faithfulness of God and the response of faith seen in Abraham and Jesus.

Claudius had expelled the Jews from Rome in 49 C.E. Later Nero softened the ban and allowed them to return. But since the Gentile Christians had enjoyed a certain degree of acceptability in Rome, the returning Jews were less than warmly welcomed since they could only draw attention to the Jewishness of the Gentile congregations, and that could only spell trouble. There therefore existed a sense of rivalry between these groups.

The importance of this fact becomes more apparent when we remember that the early Christians did not regard themselves as a new religion, nor did they draw a boundary between their beliefs and the beliefs of Judaism. As Jacob Neusner has written, the war resulting in the destruction of the Temple was the beginning of the separation between Judaism and the Christian sect.[1] These early Christians — both Christian Jews and Gentile Christians — remained loyal to the Temple and synagogue until at least 70 C.E. Even following the persecutions surrounding the destruction of the Temple, the worship of these developing Christian communities was built around the forms already established in the synagogue. They gathered for witness and worship of God as revealed through the patriarchs, prophets, and Jesus.

Sabbath-Keeping

The Jewishness of the early Christian movement can be seen in the issue of Sabbath observance. There is sufficient evidence to say that the adoption of Sunday observance by Christians did not occur until sometime around the year 135, although there was a movement for Sunday observances at least from the time of the destruction of the Temple. According to Samuele Bacchiocchi, this change originated in Rome, not in Jerusalem.[2] Indeed,

> the orthodox Palestinian Jewish-Christian sect of Nazarenes, who most scholars regard as "the very direct descendants of the primitive community" of Jerusalem, retained Sabbath-keeping on Saturday until the fourth century. Indeed, Saturday Sabbath-keeping was regarded as one of this church's distinguishing characteristics.[3]

Why did this change from Saturday to Sunday occur? After 135, when Jerusalem became a Roman colony, Jews and Christian Jews were excluded and Sabbath observances were especially condemned. In order to avoid persecutions arising over Jewish identifications, Christians changed to the Roman observance of worship on Sunday, a day set apart by Rome for the cult of *Sol Invictus*, the Invincible Sun. Although the early church leaders frequently condemned sun worship, their liturgy and thought were deeply influenced by it.

> In early Christian art and literature, the sun is often used as a symbol to represent Christ. The orientation of early Christian churches was changed; instead of facing Jerusalem like synagogues, churches were oriented to the East. The...birthday of the Invincible Sun was chosen as the Christian Christmas.[4]

The argument about the resurrection of Christ influencing the day of worship is greatly exaggerated. As Bacchiocchi argues, although "the event is greatly exalted in the New Testament, there is no hint suggesting that the event is to be celebrated at a specific time."[5] Pointing to Paul's comments to the Corinthians about the Lord's Supper, he writes that it "was initially celebrated at *indeterminate* times and commemorated Christ's death and parousia rather than his resurrection."[6] And Easter "initially celebrated

Christ's passion and was observed by the fixed date of Nisan 15 rather than on Sunday."[7]

The designation of the "first" day of the week was changed during the second century from Saturday to Sunday. With the Christian adoption of Sunday for their worship, it was clearly demonstrated "to non-Christian Romans the Christian similarity to familiar Roman practice and the dissimilarity to Jewish custom."

The anti-Judaic character of this second-century move is documented in the writings of the early leaders of the church. Justin Martyr spoke of Sabbath worship as a temporary Mosaic ordinance laid upon Jews "as a mark to single them out for the punishment they so well deserve for their infidelities."[9] The Church then changed Saturday from a joyful feast day to a sad feast day. As Pope Sylvester (314–335) wrote, this Saturday fast was not only to show sorrow for Christ's death but to show "contempt for the Jews"; Victorinus (c. 304) said that Sunday worship would help avoid "appearing to observe the Sabbath with the Jews."[10]

While it is evident to most that Christianity is a direct outgrowth of Judaism, it is not always admitted or recognized that

> the Judaism of the age of early Christianity was not the religion of Hebrew Scriptures, but rather the Judaism of an age in which Scripture was already ancient, already a legacy from the bygone past. It was a Judaism into which new institutions and new ideas had come into being.[11]

The disciples of Jesus were all Jews and the New Testament was largely written by Jews after the ministry of Paul. Why is such an obvious fact so important? Because it was to these Jews that the vision of Isaiah and Jeremiah was turned into the commission to go to *all the world*, that is, not just to Israel but to those outside of Israel, to the Gentiles. Neither the disciples nor Paul urged Jews to abandon the worship of one God to worship another; nor did they see God as abandoning Israel. To Jews, the early Christian message was that through the witness of Jesus, God was beginning to fulfill the universal vision of the prophets.

Synagogue Judaism

Christianity did not arise out of just any form of Judaism, but most likely from Synagogue Judaism. The temple worship of biblical worship with its high priest and animal sacrifices was already in a state of decline by the time of Jesus, and the practices of the relatively new institution of the synagogue had taken on new importance. Sandmel includes in Synagogue Judaism

> the visions of the apocalyptists, the idiosyncrasies of the Qumran community, and the acute legal disputes of the various Rabbinic sages. The diversities within Synagogue Judaism included matters of theological differences, messianic entanglements, and divergencies respecting details of inferences about laws and practices.[12]

The growth of the synagogue and the various cultural influences upon it were bound to be present since Jews outside Judea outnumbered those in Judea by as much as ten to one.[13] Indeed, writes Sandmel, "in the first Christian century many, many more Jews lived in the Greek world than in Judea; indeed, there were more in the city of Alexandria, Egypt...than in the Holy Land."[14]

The Exile

In order to see the growing strength of Synagogue Judaism, we need to see its rise in light of the Babylonian exile. According to Foerster, those deported were settled mainly in the area around Nippur and, as tenant-farmers, enjoyed certain limited rights: "They could acquire property, hold meetings, and even correspond with people left in Judea. Family and tribal ties, along with their natural social structure, were preserved."[15] In the Midrash on Song of Solomon (VII:8) the rabbis declared that "in exile Israel was delivered from the evil impulse to idolatry." And Zechariah (1:6) saw it as the opportunity for a movement to repentance. Bruce Vawter, abstracting an article by the French theologian Leo Laberge, writes:

> The rupture caused by the conquest of Jerusalem and the destruction of the temple in 587 [B.C.E.], then the exile and restoration in 535 and 515, transformed the life and thought of ancient Israel. The monarchy disappeared, prophecy became rare, priests and levites acquired new roles. The spirit of God inspired totally new orientations. Historically, Judaism was born of this transformation.[16]

This transformation was seen by Zechariah as a movement to repentance. On the basis of that repentance Ezra II reports that some 50,000 exiles returned to Jerusalem shortly before 520 B.C.E. Especially for the first five thousand who returned with Ezra, this meant a real sacrifice "for they were venturing into the wretched living conditions and manifold difficulties of life in Judea."[17] Of those who remained in Babylon, many sent contributions of money and goods to Jerusalem.

After a long and difficult journey of four months, it is doubtful that "they encountered any signal signs of God's favour to encourage them.... Not a vestige of political independence was granted them, and until the time of Nehemiah they apparently formed part of the area under the Persian governor in Samaria."[18] And so although they returned to Jerusalem (the limit of "greater Jerusalem" was the distance that could be reached by a day's march in any direction), they still lived under foreign rule.

The prophet Ezekiel tells that those in exile could think only in terms of restoring the old, even though in reality they could not return to the religion of their foreparents with its sacrificial system. And as time progressed, the Babylonian experience saw the links with the past slowly beginning to dissolve. Babylon was the womb in which the synagogue was being born.

This return from exile must also be seen in light of the Persian religious situation. While political autonomy did not exist among the peoples of the empire, they were nevertheless encouraged to worship their own gods for the sake of the Persian empire. Although Zoroastrianism was the official religion of the empire, it was believed that the gods of subject nations were among the helpers of Ahura Mazda, the supreme god. If these subject gods were not called upon for support, they might work against the empire. As Ellison says, "this explains the Persians' spirit of real religious tolerance within the empire. It enabled a Jewish religious community to be re-established with Jerusalem as its centre."[19]

Archaeologists tell us that Nebuchadnezzar placed the images of captured gods in the Temple of Marduk in Babylon. This included the vessels from the Temple in Jerusalem.[20] Such a display of captured gods and religious vessels demonstrated that the chief god of Babylon was superior over all these other gods, and that Ahura Mazda could then draw from their strength. However, Nebuchadnezzar's display was not totally welcomed:

He infuriated the priests of Marduk by this, and also apparently by changes in the ritual of Marduk. [Because of this] they betrayed Babylon into Cyrus' hands. Evidently part of their compact was that these gods should be sent home, not merely Marduk's "guests" but also those he had conquered. This Cyrus did at once, and where the sanctuaries had been destroyed, those that had been deported were allowed to go home to rebuild the temples.[21]

Of those returning, one in six were connected with the temple, and of this number four-fifths were priests. From this fact we might surmise that there might have been no return "had there not been so many priests who longed once more to fulfill the task in society to which they had been called by God. On the other hand the low number of Levites shows how they had gradually been squeezed out of their proper place in worship and teaching by the priests."[22]

Ezra implies (3:3) that under the conditions of the exile many Jews had ceased to see any spiritual purpose in the sacrifices for which the Temple was the symbol. This is important in understanding the New Testament. Ezra's concept of the law was itself tempered by the times. For him,

the keeping of the Torah did not merely mean the carrying out of what was expressly commanded in the Pentateuch. It did not even mean conforming to the interpretation which Ezra, with the power of the Persian state behind him, pronounced as official. It involved the applying of these principles to every conceivable aspect of life, even if they were unknown in the time of Moses.[23]

Such thinking would have been opposed by the priests who were the guardians of tradition. In addition, it would have been opposed by the city's wealthy families since "it placed the poorer citizen religiously on the same level as the noble and rich."[24]

By the beginning of the third century B.C.E., Ptolemy, Alexander's personal staff-officer, emerged as the governor of Egypt and later "annexed Palestine and Coele-Syria to act as a shield for his desert frontier."[25] Josephus tells how

Ptolemy deported a large number of Jews to Egypt, the majority of whom were apparently settled in Alexandria. They were not full citizens...but they were given special privileges, which proved so attractive that they were soon joined voluntarily by others. This was the beginning of the Western diaspora or dispersion, which was to play such a tremendous part in Jewish history and also in the spread of the early church.[26]

Within the next three centuries, Jerusalem was captured at least three times, and continually served under foreign domination. The struggle was always to fight against such domination and the idolatry that came with it. The attitude that came to a head in the Maccabean period reached its climax in the Zealot movement.

During the first century B.C.E., those who had kept the Law faithfully felt they could no longer blame all of their political and cultural woes on the fact that the Law had not been rightly observed. And whatever the origins of the synagogue during this time, a major reason is undoubtedly the corruption of the Temple and its services. Growing out of the experiences of the Exile when the Temple was not available and the decline in the meaning of animal sacrifices, the synagogue became an acceptable substitute. In exile the scriptures regained their dynamic quality, and Hebrew was soon replaced by the languages of Greek and Aramaic. With this change in language came also the new concepts and images of these languages. The most obvious consequence of this change, and the most devastating in connection with our present study of Romans, was that "Greek Jews gave to the Five Books the title *nomos* ("law"), a word with a ring quite different from that of *Torah* ("divine teaching").[27] Because of this change in conception of *Torah*, and because Christians based their doctrines and claims on this Greek translation, the Septuagint, the rabbis virtually disowned such changes.

Throughout this study, we must remember that Torah is a multifaceted concept which includes everything revealed by God to Israel. Importantly, this includes the oral traditions. Oral teaching made the revelation of God a dynamic force as it spoke to changing situations and gave persons guidance in how to act with justice and love in fulfillment of the divine will. Because of this dynamic quality, Torah was new with each generation. And rightly understood, Paul stands firmly in this tradition.

Christianity: Sect of Judaism

Christianity was not the only sect within Judaism to claim a new revelation or to claim to be the "true Israel" or the "new Israel." There were several such groups which grew up in the two centuries surrounding the beginning of the common era. These included Hasidim, Sadducees, Pharisees, Essenes, Zealots, Sicarii, Fourth Philosophy, Therapeutae, Ebionites, Haemerobaptists, and Christian. According to Sandmel's research,

> some eight "heresies" were counted by Epiphanies; for our purposes it is sufficient that we have an awareness of the multiplicity of these groupings, and understand that local manifestations of infinite variety were characteristic of that age in Judea.[28]

From this we must conclude that Judaism developed under many conditions, in various forms, and over an extended period of time. As James H. Charlesworth, Director of the International Center for the Study of Christian Origins at Duke University, writes:

> Working on the Pseudepigrapha, the Dead Sea Scrolls, the Apocrypha, targums, and early rabbinic writings has opened scholars' eyes to the rich varieties within Judaism before the conflagration of Jerusalem in [C.E.] 70. No longer is it wise to talk about an orthodox or monolithic Judaism; no longer is it possible to distinguish clearly between Palestinian and Diasporic Judaism. Likewise, most criteria once organized to help us distinguish between a Jewish and Christian composition have collapsed.[29]

The same divergency of thought and practice developed early among the Christian communities. Within the Christian sect of Judaism, Paul lists four groups which had formed around various leaders. He writes: "What I mean is that each one of you says, 'I belong to Paul,' or 'I belong to Apollos,' or 'I belong to Cephas,' or 'I belong to Christ'" (1 Cor. 1:12). Sandmel helps us understand what this verse probably means:

> The party of Cephas would presumably be that of the "judaizers," advocates of observing the mitzvot. Apollos is

identified in Acts 18:24-28 as a Jew of Alexandria, and possibly the party of Apollos was extremely partisan to allegory, as was Philo, and possibly espoused a contrast beyond that of Paul between "flesh" and spirit, and possibly was unconcerned about the literal traditions taught about Jesus. Possibly the "party of Christ" was even more extreme.[30]

At the time of Paul, Christianity was a sect of Judaism, growing basically out of Synagogue Judaism, and was not yet a separate institution outside of Judaism. Religious thought was in great flux during the period of Paul's ministry. However, such a rich diversity of Jewish religious expression ought not obscure the fact that

> for much of Jewish Palestine, Judaism was a relatively new phenomenon. Herod was the grandson of pagans. Similarly, the entire of Galilee had been converted to Judaism only one hundred and twenty years before the Common Era. In the later expansion of the Hasmonean kingdom, other regions were forcibly brought within the fold. The Hasmoneans used Judaism imperially, as a means of winning the loyalty of the pagan Semites in the regions of Palestine they conquered.[31]

Judaism, then, was used much like Constantine used later Christianity as a secular religion for bringing all the people under his rule. However, such forced conversions do not easily transform one's commitments from former cultural ideas and practices to the new one. Rather, all forms and ideas are to some extent synthesized. This fact is important to remember in order not to lump all groups into the same mold.

The relationship between Judaism and Greek culture might be well illustrated by focusing on the concept of God. Biblical theology is relational and employs anthropomorphisms not to define the *nature* of God but to describe the *relationship* of God with creation. Thus, God is known according to perceived divine activity. One part of this concept of God which the rabbis held in common with Greek culture is also seen in Paul: knowledge of the true God was possible even for the heathen, although that knowledge may be quite limited in scope.

Because Temple Judaism dealt so much with the legal aspects of cult and ritual, the rise of the synagogue began to answer the needs of many Galileans who were so recently converted to

Judaism, and of the common people whose daily toil allowed so little time or inclination for the cultic law. Gentile proselytes attached themselves to the Jewish community but were put off by adult male circumcision. Indeed, as Cook points out, "the extremely rapid Helenization of Christianity is in large measure traceable to inroads made by Jewish proselytism."[32] The new Christian sect, with its claim that Gentiles need not be circumcised, became attractive to many who had attached themselves to the beliefs and practices of Diaspora Judaism. Indeed, Judaism in Diaspora actually paved the way for the Christian sect's later success with Gentiles. Had it not been for the Jewish emphasis on circumcision, the results of Christian history would have undoubtedly concluded quite differently.

Paul: A Christian Jewish Missionary

Paul was born in Tarsus, a part of Diaspora Judaism. It is probable that one of his ancestors settled in Tarsus in the second century B.C.E. Antiochus III (223-187 B.C.E.), "after he had won Palestine from the Ptolemies, caused his general Zeuxis to send two thousand Jewish families from Mesopotamia and Babylonia to Lydia and Phrygia, where there had been plots against him, because he knew he could count on Jewish loyalty."[33] His successor, Antiochus IV, followed the same policy of forced migration but sweetening this bitterness by granting them many communal rights along with full citizenship. Ellison says of these persons:

> It may be because full citizenship brought them into closer contact with their Hellenized, pagan fellow-citizens, it may be because they were moved so suddenly to an ancient area of Greek culture, they were more than most out of touch with Jerusalem. Here, and virtually here alone in dispersion, we find evidence for the syncretistic influenced introduced by Hellenism.... Probably there was a greater acceptance of the gospel by Jews in this area than anywhere else.[34]

Paul was raised in this atmosphere in the ways of Pharisaism and under the influence of the relatively new and developing synagogue system. This fact is important in understanding Paul's association with the Christian sect. The Pharisaism under which Paul was trained was probably different from that which we find in Palestine.

Its interaction with Greek culture certainly produced its own character, and it was this special character that would have determined Paul's own thinking. This much can be said about the Greek influence on Judaism:

> The Pentateuch was a Greek work of law, revealing a God of refined philosophic reason, and suffused with philosophic concerns: Logos...universals and particulars, causality, chance and fate, the individual's plight, resurrection, immortality, and the like. Its specific laws enabled individual man to triumph over his passions, ensuring his soul's escape from bondage and attainment of life eternal in the realm of the incorporeal.[35]

According to Foerster, this Greek influence led to a "neglect of the historical" with a concurrent emphasis on ceremony. And according to Sandmel, this Greek influence was so much accepted by Jews that they were occasionally embarrassed to find that scripture and the Greek philosophers were saying the same thing.[36] When Paul is compared to Jews such as Philo rather than to the Old Testament or to Palestinian Judaism, he does not seem so distant from his Jewish background. It is the contention of this work that Paul's arguments are not directed against Judaism as such, but against certain distortions or Greek reinterpretations of it.

This fact alone must cause us to look again at Paul's Road-to-Damascus experience. Scripture gives four accounts of this experience — three from the traditions reported by Luke and one which Paul gives himself. It will be demonstrated in this study that it is wrong to consider this Road-to-Damascus experience as a "conversion" in the usual sense. To do so would obligate us to consider the experiences of Isaiah and Jeremiah, as well as scores of others, as conversions. With Stendahl we should speak of Paul's "call" to a very specific vocation, that is, to proclaim that God's justification and salvation are for all people of the earth. His efforts in that mission to the Gentiles are to reflect the promises of Isaiah and Jeremiah. He is now an "apostle to the Gentiles," i.e., a Jewish missionary. This is supported also by the fact that when Paul refers to "our" and "we" he consistently means "we Jews" as opposed to "you Gentiles." And he constantly cites Old Testament passages to support his claims of inclusiveness.

Paul's Judaism is not unique, even with his christological additions. Many of the issues with which he deals were also dealt with by Philo and other Jews. The question of the "value, relevancy, and claim to eminence of the Law of Moses"[37] were already being debated by Jews in dispersion as well as by Philo. For Paul as well as for Philo, "the Messianic activity...would be 'cosmic' rather than national." The difference was that "Palestinian Jews saw in the Messiah the divine agent who would help the collective people out of their national predicament, while Paul [and Philo] saw in him the means of the salvation of individuals out of the human predicament."[38]

Paul and Philo also agree (against the rabbinic contention) that God continues divine revelation into the present, and that revelation did not cease "with Ezra in the fifth pre-Christian century."[39] Paul and Philo both called into question the relationship of "the law and the prophets." "The traditional order had been predicated on the assumption that the fount of prophetic inspiration had dried up...and that the prophetic word survived only in written word."[40] They question whether Torah is rightly defined as only law, and therefore whether God is primarily a lawgiver or judge.

Traditional Christian theology makes the same mistake as did those with whom Paul quarreled. It, too, has equated the whole of the Old Testament with law, and with the companion concept of God as judge and lawgiver. By doing so Christianity has failed to see that Gospel is also a part of the Old Testament just as law and judgment are a part of the New Testament. We need only to see the Gospel of the covenant as the gracious action of a gracious God.

Stendahl also helps us to see that Paul is not plagued by guilt and introspection, nor does he plead with either Jew or Gentile to feel an anguished conscience in order for them to receive forgiveness and release from that anguish. Even the law is not given in order to make us feel guilty, but is a gracious gift of God for the ordering of life until the arrival of the fullness of God's kingdom. This is essential for us to understand since faith for Paul is a change from self-trust to confidence in the leading and faithfulness of God.

As we attempt to see Paul as a Christian Jewish missionary, we need to be aware of how translators have unwittingly inserted their own bias into the Scripture. Ernest Saunders has discovered in the letter of James, a basically Jewish tract, an interesting refusal to recognize the character of the early Christian community:

> Deploring the extension of a pagan caste system into the church, James wrote, "If a man with gold rings and in fine

clothing comes into your *synagogue* (= Aramaic *k'nishta*),"
you are not to show him any deferential treatment (Jas 2:2).
Later the writer uses the more familiar Greek word for church,
ekklesia (5:14). But in view of the fact that Jewish-Christians re-
tained the word "synagogue" for their own meetings and
meeting-places, the singular use of that word in the letter is
worthy of note.[41]

We are so prone to see the early church through the filters of
present experience, thereby seeing two very distinct groups — Jews
and Christians. Even Saunders' use of the phrase "Jewish-Christians"
betrays this. We prefer to use the designation "Christian Jews" as
being more in line with the facts and situation of the early church
prior to the destruction of the Temple. Scholars are discovering
more about the sectarian nature of Judaism in these times. As Rabbi
Phillip Sigal writes:

> The present generation, which witnesses at least five "official"
> denominations (Reconstructionist, Reform, Conservative,
> Orthodox, Hasidic), is far overshadowed by the proto-rabbinic
> society of the first centuries B.C.E. and C.E. when, we are in-
> formed, there were at least twenty-four denominations.[42]

Despite the fact that Sandmel states that there were almost four
times that number does not alter the point.
    Traditional theology points to the Road-to-Damascus experi-
ence as Paul's conversion from the religion of Judaism to the religion of Christianity. However, upon closer examination in terms of
the actual situation of the day, it is more honest to speak of Paul's
experience as a call from one level of faith to a higher level of faith.
Paul began to see that God's promises were extended to all. Thus,
Paul received a call into the service of a new level of witness as
reflected in the promises of Isaiah and Jeremiah. God's messiah had
now asked him as a Jew to bring the gospel of God to the Gentiles.
    In answering this call, Paul did not abandon the rich theology
of the Patriarchs, but rather sought to give it a deeper meaning in
light of the witness of Jesus. To reinforce this stance in his letters,
he used the mutually supporting terminology of grace and peace in
each of his greetings: "Grace and peace be unto you from God our
Father and the Lord Jesus Christ." Grace refers to the graciousness
of God as seen in the faithfulness of God in the past and as presently

seen in the witness of Jesus, that is, the extension of the patriarchal promises to the Gentiles. Grace, then, reflects the new Christian tradition. Peace, on the other hand, reflects the rich concept of *Shalom* and the promises of Judaism for the whole world. By using these two terms together, Paul provides a basis of authority for his message that designated the continuity of Jewish promise and Christian inclusiveness.

Paul used the term "all" more than forty-seven times in Romans alone to drive home the point that Jews and Gentiles alike are justified by God. The boundaries which previously separated them have now been abolished by an act of God in Jesus Christ. Paul refers to this unity as he states the meaning of his apostleship:

> God's grace made me a *minister* of Jesus Christ *to the gentiles*; my *priestly service* is the preaching of the *gospel of God*, and it falls to me to offer the gentiles to God as an acceptable sacrifice, consecrated by his Holy Spirit (Rom 15:16).

Traditional interpreters of Christianity argue that Paul could not have been a Christian Jewish missionary since Judaism has never been a missionary religion in the common sense of the term. All readily agree that Judaism had been called to be a divine witness among the nations, although the witness was made passively. However, recent research has given us a different understanding of Judaism during the centuries surrounding the beginning of the common era. Rabbi Bokser tells us that "Jewish religious tradition found its formal crystallization in the Pharisaic-rabbinic period, and one of its active concerns was to wage an active campaign to disseminate its teachings throughout the world."[43] This missionary movement did not insist on conversion as such. They sought not to make Jews, but to share their revelation of God's good news. Conversion assumes an exclusivistic understanding that one's own religious expression is the only one that possesses the keys to salvation. And while every religious expression tends in this direction, this missionary movement was not presented in such a manner. Rather, it saw the rites and rituals of Judaism "as channels of a transcendent light, as vessels containing a truth which resides in them and is cultivated through them, but that truth has a life of its own that is capable of reaching and enriching other lives outside its own system."[44] Indeed, says Rabbi Bokser, "these Jewish missionaries often dissuaded a would-be convert from formal initiation into Judaism. They counseled him, instead, to remain in his own household of faith but to live by the light of the Jewish principles which transcended the formalism in its rites and ceremonies."[45] According to Rabbi Moskowitz, this movement took as its basis Leviticus 19:34:

> When a stranger (*ger*) resides with you in your land, you shall not wrong him. The stranger who resides with you shall be to you one of your citizens; you shall love him as yourself, for you were strangers in the land of Egypt; I am the Lord your God.

In this context "*ger* referred to a foreign-born alien who sought to cast his lot with the early Hebrews."[46] The development of this missionary spirit must be seen from at least three points. First, the words of Moses recorded in Leviticus set the stage. "It is not only because they themselves were once the alien people, but also because he, himself, was once a *ger* and has himself, in fact, married a foreign woman."[47]

The second point is the influence of the Ezra-Nehemiah period with its attempt to cleanse the Jewish nation of its foreign elements, including wives and children. This must be seen in its historical context when "the cultural decadence of the Jews had reached the level where they 'could no longer speak the language of Judah'."[48]

But by the time we get to the years surrounding the beginning of the common era,

> direct and continual contacts with divergent peoples, the dynamic force of Hellenism with its inducements, and the pre-Constantinian tolerance of certain Roman emperors brought about a physical and spiritual expansion of Judaism, a feeling of universalism and missionary zeal hitherto unknown in the Jewish community.[49]

Moskowitz says that "it is in this spirit that one can perhaps appreciate the Talmudic statement that the Jews were exiled for the expressed purpose of collecting proselytes."[50]

Paul's understanding of apostleship clearly reflects the missionary concern of his time. His constant theme is also their theme: the faithfulness of God with the supreme human response being circumcision of the heart. We are then led to conclude that his Road-to-Damascus experience was not a change from faithlessness to faith, from immorality to morality, nor even from a sinful state to a state of salvation. His experience was one of change in direction in his *ministry*, not in his *priesthood* (Rom 15:16). It was a change from a ministry directed solely to his fellow Jews to a ministry of reconciliation to all persons and especially to the Gentiles.

Paul eventually came to believe that the essential aspect of Jewish rite was in the spiritual meaning rather than its physical application. This is not to say that he ignored the physical. If we are to believe Luke's account of the circumcision of Timothy, then Paul continued to perform these rites even after he had won the argument at the Jerusalem Council against the necessity of physical circumcision. And while it is true that in Romans Paul refers to those who need the assurance of rite and ritual as "weak in faith," he nowhere suggests that these persons should give up such practices. His basic argument was not against the rites as such but against their necessity for justification and salvation. He carefully instructed those he considered "strong in faith" not to offend the sensitivities of the others who were also brothers and sisters in faith.

In this way, Paul assured his fellow Jews that God had not abandoned them but had only drawn a larger circle to include the Gentiles as the prophets had promised. He argued that beginning with Abraham the unity of all persons as children of God has been based on faith in God alone. God is not fickle. His promise to Abraham had not been invalidated by the coming of Jesus. Rather, the promise had been fulfilled in his witness. God is faithful. This faithfulness has now been guaranteed to *all* who hold faith in God. There is, therefore, no discontinuity between true Judaism as reflected in Abraham and true Christianity as reflected in Jesus, "for the righteousness of God is revealed through faith for faith" (Rom 1:17). The foundation for all faith is the faithfulness of God.

Because Christians have consistently misunderstood Paul's Road-to-Damascus experience, they have failed to see Paul's Jewishness in his later ministry. Christians have also misunderstood the debate over circumcision in this time-period. Most have claimed that Paul set out to deliberately destroy this rite. However, since Paul knew the rite to be a sign of God's covenant with Israel, he did not despise it, but only said that the new rite of baptism was more appropriate for Gentile Christians. But *neither* of these rites could justify or save! To continue the traditional argument that

Paul set out to abolish circumcision is to also undermine all Christian rites. If God had a change of mind about Jews and the value of circumcision, is it not also most probable that God might also have a change of mind in the future — this time about Christians and their sacraments? Indeed, if God is not faithful to Jews, Christians will also find themselves cut off!

Paul's aim, then, was to set Jewish rite and ritual in prophetic perspective. This struggle over circumcision is more easily understood when we see the emotions surrounding the issue in the prior two centuries. By the time of the Maccabees, circumcision had taken on the essential meaning of national unity and confession of faith for which one was willing to die. Antiochus IV not only deported thousands of Jews, but also persecuted those who remained.

> In accordance with the royal decree, they put to death women and those who had had their children circumcised. Their babies, their families, and those who had circumcised them, they hanged by the neck. Yet many in Israel found strength to resist.... *They welcomed death rather than defile themselves and profane the holy covenant,* and so they died (1 Macc 1:60–64).

Many in those two centuries leading up to this time had given their lives to preserve this holy covenant between themselves and God. Some gave up the practice and fled from Jerusalem. But as they went, they took with them the seeds of faith. They carried with them the idea that if the holy covenant was not to be profaned completely, some reinterpretation would be necessary which would include the intent of the rite without relying on the external form. Many found this option in the prophetic writings, and their descendants welcomed Paul's reinterpretation which he based on Jeremiah's vision.

When we put all of this together with Paul's own illustration of the Olive Tree, wherein the new Christian sect is shown to be a branch of Judaism and Christians are said to be "honorary Jews," we are then confronted with the central issue of christology versus theology. We must remember that Paul is a Christian Jew, not a Jewish Christian. How, then, are we to understand Paul's expression of faith in Jesus Christ?

Faith in Jesus Christ and salvation through Christ Jesus are phrases used in reference to the terms "example," "type," and "foreshadowing." For the Gentile, it was the example seen in Jesus that makes them heirs of God's promises with Jews. To Jews, this type of faith seen in Jesus reinforced the original idea that it is by faith that one is justified.

Dr. Calvin Porter of Christian Theological Seminary has suggested that the phrase, "faith *in* Christ Jesus," is poorly translated and is another instance of the bias of traditional translation. Instead, the phrase might better read, "faith *of* Christ Jesus." Porter points out that the Greek genative case is used here in the same way as in Romans 4:4 where the same word order is translated, "faith *of* Abraham." The translation, "in," is based on a later high christological tradition. Viewed in this manner, the meaning of these various phrases becomes consistent with the character of Paul as a Christian Jew, and it ties together with Jesus' own witness that the purpose of his own life was not to draw attention to himself but to point persons toward God.

Further, since Paul is very concerned with all forms of idolatry, it is highly doubtful that he would in any way equate God with the human life of Jesus. His reference, then, is not faith in Jesus to the exclusion of faith in God, or even equation of the one with the other, but a faith that in Jesus God has been revealed in a universally significant manner. If one prefers to maintain the confusing usage of "faith *in* Christ Jesus," which most will certainly do for traditional reasons, it needs to be realized that faith in Christ does *not* carry the same material significance as faith in God. To allow the two to become equivalent is idolatrous.

Messianic Hope

Generally speaking, Jews in these years surrounding the start of the common era expected a messiah to come, but this messianic appearance was not an absolute necessity. God works in many ways, and not always in the manner expected. Rivkin tells us that prior to the time of Jesus, "no messianic claim had survived the death of the would-be Messiah."[51]

The concept of a messiah appears to have "emerged spontaneously as a solution to a series of problems that Judaism had to face in the Greco-Roman world, problems for which there were no direct solutions in the Pentateuch."[52] This crisis also produced a new class of leaders—the Pharisees, or as they called themselves,

Soferim. Because of the politicizing of the office of High Priest, several persons who had bought the office tried to Hellenize it. This produced a severe loss of confidence, and without trustworthy and legitimate temple authorities, the Pharisees stepped in to fill the void. They claimed that God gave not only the written law but also the oral law, both of which they were now the legitimate interpreters. And the majority of the people were with them. Resenting the mass corruption of the temple offices by usurpers, they gave this authority informally to the Pharisees.

The Pharisees paved the way for the ideas of the later Christian movement to take form. They proclaimed that God was "the Heavenly Father of the individual." They also proclaimed the good news of "personal salvation, of eternal life, or resurrection, transmuted the concept of the peoplehood of Israel, and the relationship of this people to both God and to the Holy Land."[53] Because of these particular novel teachings, "the divine promises were transferred from the nation and the Land to the individual. Salvation depended on adherence to the system of the two-fold law and not on birth."[54] This meant that salvation could be offered to the Gentiles as the prophets had proclaimed. For this reason, the Pharisees began the missionary movement with which Paul was to become associated.

Since salvation did not depend on the land, the temple, the nation, or birth, the idea of a messiah became expendable. "So long as the road to salvation was not blocked by insuperable obstacles in this world, all that was necessary was the two-fold law and the firm belief that adherence to it would yield salvation."[55] Therefore, the thing that made the idea of a crucified messiah acceptable at all was the Pharisaic concept of the resurrection of the dead, the new spiritual form of reward once the idea of messiah was no longer tied to a territorial future.

Then why did Paul so zealously persecute Christian Jews in his early ministry? Rivkin offers the following partial answer:

> Was it not because Paul's personal salvation was at stake? The Pharisees proclaimed the gospel of God the Father. They taught the two-fold Law as His revelation. They promised eternal life and resurrection to the faithful and the obedient. Resurrection was the reward for loyal Jews. No one could be resurrected who had been disloyal. Yet the disciples of Jesus preached Jesus as the resurrected Christ, the very Jesus who had, in his life-

time, set himself up as a law unto himself. He had challenged
the Pharisees and defied them.... Now his disciples were proclaiming that this challenger of Pharisaic authority had risen
from the dead. This could not be! Resurrection was the reward
for obedience, not rebellion.[56]

Believing that Christians were undermining the Law, they
sought to destroy the force of the movement. Here we must
remember that it was not all Jews, not even all Pharisees, who were
persecuting this Christian sect. It was only among the more
zealous. And had not Jesus urged his followers to accept the word
of the Pharisees as normative in regards to the Law? Indeed, the
standard for measuring righteousness in the new Christian sect was
to be the Pharisaic standard (Mt 5:17–20; 23:2). Jesus himself was
undoubtedly trained in the Pharisaic traditions and was himself a
Pharisee.

Remembering that the Pharisees had introduced the change
which affirmed that law and not birth was the thing that tied the
community of faith together, we see Paul struggling with varying
ideas of what the messiah was to be. If there is to be a messiah,
he concluded, then the concept must be redefined which takes this
spiritualizing process into account, and the messiah internalized.

This internalization is clear in Paul's discussion of the messiah
or Christ. No longer is the messiah a savior of the people through
territorial promise but a savior of individuals. No longer is the
messiah a warrior-king of God's choice, but rather the spiritual
function of God that abides within every person of faith. Paul is
nowhere concerned with the historical Jesus, but focuses on the
risen, exalted, or internalized Christ as the mode of God's
revelation.

Proof-Texting Method

A final word needs to be said concerning Paul's usage of scripture. His method is what we commonly refer to as proof-texting. It
is no longer accepted as a valid means of interpreting scripture
except by some of the more fundamentalist groups. While the
Pharisees did not deny the validity of the Pentateuch, they did
argue that the same authority belonged to the Oral Law. They were
thus committed to the principle of continual revelation. Since Jesus

was most probably a Pharisee, and in any case did demand that his disciples follow the teachings of the Pharisees, then we must conclude that neither was Jesus a biblical literalist.

Rivkin tells us that the proof-texting method of biblical interpretation was a radical innovation which the Pharisees made in Judaism, although it was common in the historical and philosophical writings of the Greco-Roman world. When Paul used this method, it was one that he had learned in his religious training.

> ...the fact that Paul utilizes the very same proof-texting mode as that found in the Mishnah, without any qualification, and since this proof-texting mode is non-Pentateuchal and non-scriptural, it bespeaks the revolutionary activity of the Pharisees as having occurred long before his day.[57]

Rivkin then described how this innovation took place. First, although God is said to have chosen Aaron to be "the father of an eternal priesthood," the same Pentateuch says that "God had chosen not Aaron's son Elsazar but a non-priest, Joshua, to succeed Moses as the leader of Israel."[58] Thus, is was the prophet-like figure rather than the priesthood in which God had invested authority.

Second, the Pharisees demonstrated how these prophetic leaders "had again and again carried out actions or issued commands that were at variance with the Written Law."[59] Since the prophets were regarded as spokesmen for Yahweh, their deeds and words became unwritten laws.

Third, they pointed out "the many contradictions within the Pentateuch itself which allowed for alternative options."[60] Fourth, and closely related with the third, the Pharisees took advantage "of the inherent ambiguity of language, insisting that the meaning could be 'this' rather than 'that'."[61]

Fifth, they confronted the Aaronide priests "with procedures and practices that were in vogue and taken for granted but which were not explicitly written down in the Pentateuch."[62] The priests claimed that these procedures were obvious inferences. The Pharisees claimed that they were evidence of unwritten law.

And sixth, their method of proof-texting "shattered the contextual matrix" of scripture:

> A biblical verse was considered to be a discrete entity, which could be lifted out of context and utilized as a meaning in itself.

It could thus be used, either alone or in linkage with other biblical verses, as proof of a law or a doctrine. As such it was immune to challenge from the verse which preceded and followed. Scripture thus became a veritable arsenal, bristling with verses which could be used with lethal effect against the Sadducees.[63]

Through this innovation the Pharisees revealed the road to eternal life. They called their innovation *halakhuh*, "the way," which oddly enough was the name chosen by the first Christians to describe their sect.

With this important background in mind, let us look at Paul's letter to the Romans.

1

One or More Congregations?

The first issue with which we must deal in our study of Paul's letter to the Romans is whether he was addressing one congregation in Rome, several congregations in Rome, or congregations in several cities with Rome being only one of its recipients. We shall attempt to demonstrate in this chapter that Paul is addressing several congregations in Rome.

The cosmopolitan nature of the city undoubtedly affected the character of the congregations there. There were more than eleven synagogues in the city, and the congregations with which Paul is corresponding is just as diverse. From even a hurried skimming of Romans, we can see that the congregations differ over holy days, circumcision, dietary rules, openness of the common meal and worship—with the basic overarching debate surrounding the superiority of scripture (i.e., Jewish law and custom, and Torah) versus the superiority of tradition (i.e., the new slant of the Christian message).

The answer to the question suggested by this chapter is found in Minear's examination of Romans 16.[1] Most commentators see this chapter as part of a letter to the church at Ephesus which was later attached to this letter to the Romans in order that it not be lost. Others say that it was a copy of the general letter that went to Ephesus. Still others see it as a latter addition to Romans.

However, if we accept Romans 16 as part of the original letter, we begin to discover that there are at least five house-congregations in Rome, with at least one being set up by Christian Jews who had returned to Rome after being expelled by the emperor Claudius in 49 C.E. These congregations most probably met in the homes of the following persons:

1. Prisca (Priscilla) and Aquila. They are husband and wife who were expelled from Rome by Claudius and at the time of this letter were risking their lives by returning to Rome to help establish Paul's ministry and to prepare the way for his visit. They are Christian Jews who were enough respected in Rome to give Paul a letter of recommendation as he traveled from Ephesus to Achaia, north of Corinth. Aquila, like Paul, was a tent-maker.

2. Aristobulus. Legend says that he was one of the seventy disciples sent out by Jesus. He is also credited with being one of the first Christian missionaries to Britain.

3. Asyncritus. Nothing is known of this person.

4. Narcissus. Legend has it that he was a favorite slave of the emperor Claudius who had been freed.

5. Philologus. Nothing is known of this person.

Most helpful to us in this study are the five faith stances found within these congregations in Rome. They are certainly mixed in with one another to some extent, but each faith group had a different emphasis. Minear suggests the following basic positions which are addressed by Paul in this letter to the Romans.[2]

FIRST, the "weak in faith" who condemn the "strong in faith." These persons declare that God has announced in Moses and the prophets what must be done, and those who deviate from "God's standards" will not be saved. They assume the right and duty of both defining and enforcing these rules of behavior. They do not view all days as sacred, but hold to the Sabbath. Likewise, they make distinctions between good and bad foods and drinks based on the dietary laws, and they condemn as sinners anyone who does not agree with them. They are called "weak" by Paul because he did not consider their faith sufficiently strong or secure or "freed-up" to overcome their "bondage to the law."

SECOND, the "strong in faith" who condemn the "weak in faith." This group, like the first, considered itself superior over those who disagreed with their interpretations. Not only do they enjoy arguing with the "weak," they despise them. These persons declare that they are free to eat and drink anything since Christ has liberated them from all laws and regulations. They are suspicious of any who would try to re-establish religious obligations and restrictions. They do not abide by Jewish ritual and custom, and scorn all who do. Käsemann points out that it is this group with whom Paul is most concerned. He writes that it is characteristic of Paul's theology "to be seldom concerned with our deficiencies and weaknesses.... Unlike the usual sermon, the apostle is exceptionally unconcerned with our definciencies; his attacks are directed against the strong." And why should this be so? Because for Paul, the strong person "is always the representative of the world and its religiosity, where these are at their most interesting and at the same time most deeply compromised."³

THIRD, the "doubters." This group represents the middle-of-the-roaders, those who are not clear about what is right to do. They are pulled between both the weak and the strong, but usually give in to the security of a double safety of legal righteousness. They tend to act without reference to a faith stance, without appealing to conscience, and therefore only react to social pressures within the community.

FOURTH, the "weak in faith" who do *not* condemn the "strong in faith." This group holds to the Jewish definition of right behavior and religious observance without condemning those who disagree. They have accepted the Gospel of Jesus that the Kingdom of God is for all who have faith in God, but insist that Gentiles should demonstrate this faith in refusing to eat foods sacrificed to idols, meat that has been killed by strangulation, the eating or drinking of blood, and all forms of unchastity (i.e., fornication, with specific reference to pagan forms of prostitution).

And FIFTH, the "strong in faith" who do *not* condemn the "weak in faith." Paul classifies himself in this group. While maintaining that Christ has freed them from the bondage of law and ritual, these persons forgo personal freedoms necessary in order to extend hospitality to the "weak." Therefore, every particular situation must determine its own specific behavior as long as it is within the encompassing law of love for God and neighbor. This is summed up in Paul's words: "Then let us no more pass judgment on one another, but rather decide never to put a stumbling block or hinderance in the way of a brother [or sister]; let each of us please his neighbor for his good, to edify him. For Christ did not please himself" (14:13; 15:2–3a).

With these particular distinctions in mind, we will move into our study of the text of Romans. We will follow the natural divisions of the letter as suggested by Minear⁴ based on the above stated faith stances. That division is as follows:

I 1:1–17   To all readers, but with distinctions made

II 1:18–4:15   To the weak in faith who condemn the strong in faith

III	4:16–5:21	To all readers, but with distinctions made
IV	6:1–23	To the strong in faith who condemn the weak in faith
V	7:1–8:8	To the weak in faith who condemn the strong in faith
VI	8:9–11:12	To the doubters
VII	11:13–13:14	To the strong in faith who condemn the weak in faith
VIII	14:1–15:32	Alternating between the weak, the strong, and the doubters
IX	16:1–27	To all readers

2

All One in Faith

Early in his ministry as a Christian Jew, Paul became convinced that Gentile converts should not have to submit to the rite of circumcision. This issue led to the Jerusalem Conference where Paul debated with the followers of Peter and James. He remembered this conference as being much more important than did Luke. In Romans we see him arguing that the congregations should be open to everyone without having to observe that former sign of group membership. Everyone of faith, Jew and Gentile alike, is to be accepted into God's justification. For Paul, God has made this clear through the divine revelation in the life, death, and resurrection of Jesus Christ. Thus, the congregations' membership should be open to all, and he reinforces this in his greeting: "Grace and peace to you from God our Father and the Lord Jesus Christ" (1:7b). Here he uses the mutually supporting terminology of Jewish scripture and the new Christian tradition. "Grace," the grace of God in Jesus the Messiah, is the Christian concept. "Peace," the peace of God, shalom, is the Jewish concept. And he uses these terms in each of his letters to provide a basis of authority for what he has to say. As Ellis writes in a review article:

> He does not do this in a mechanical fashion but by an interpretive reworking of both scripture and the traditions to set forth "my gospel" (Rom 2:16; 16:25), that is, the theme of Christology and justification. In this way Paul wants to show that his specific message is not his alone, but that it stands in continuity with the Old Testament and the primitive Christian tradition.[1]

By putting the two terms together, "grace and peace," Paul is saying to his readers: "Greetings to all of you — Gentile Christians and Christian Jews alike."

The importance of this is almost lost to us today since we all too often see the early Christian congregations as separate and distinct from Judaism and the synagogue. We think in terms of the divisions between present-day Christianity and Judaism. But the separations in these first century groups were probably not all that clear. Pharisees, Sadducees, Essenes, Zealots, Christians — all could hold their differences and at the same time be held together in the same body. For the more progressive of the groups it was realized that only God had the right to accept or reject in the final analysis. This is not to say that there were not major differences, but only that these differences did not always prove alienating.

Therefore, one could acclaim Jesus as the promised messiah and at the same time remain a loyal Jew. Thus, Paul's greeting is not at all incidental to his purposes. Through the greeting Paul was saying:

> God is not revealed to only one people or one group, but has been made known to all people to some degree. The proof of whether one has accepted that revelation lies only in one's faith in God's leading. Therefore, we are freed from every boundary that formerly separated us. And if this is so, we need only live in terms of such freedom with one another.

We have then touched on Paul's major theme in the early words of the letter. Neither Jew nor Christian nor any other group is to feel superior over others in their relationship to God's justification and salvation. We are all now children of God the Father — Jew and non-Jew alike! God has brought us together in our sinfulness and in our salvation: "As in Adam *all* die, so in Christ shall *all* be made alive."

This is an essential theme for Christians to hear today. We have become extremely parochial, claiming that we alone, of all the peoples of the world, are God's chosen and therefore claim the right to demand that all must become "christian" in order to be justified and saved. Of course, after a closer reading of Romans we realize that Paul does not say that at all. Indeed, such an argument is in direct violation of what he is proclaiming. What he does announce is that salvation and justification has come to non-Jews through the vehicle of Jesus Christ from God the Father. We have all—Jew and non-Jew alike—been set free by the witness of God in the life, death, and resurrection of Jesus Christ from those boundaries that previously divided us into chosen and not chosen, saved and not saved, justified and not justified. It is in light of this that we understand Paul's apostolic mission: "To bring *all* persons of *all* nations to the *obedience of faith*." This, then, is the major message of Romans.

This letter is addressed to "All of God's beloved in Rome who are *called* to be *saints*." A saint is "one set apart for God's use."[2] This is a term used in reference to the community of faith which is called by God to be a consecrated people on behalf of the world. The saints, then, are members of the community of faith—ideally, all members—who radiate the glory of God through their obedience to God and the Kingdom of God. Their calling, therefore, implies a high ethical standard which is demonstrated through love for one another and practical service. More specifically, Paul is intent on interpreting this obedience of faith as contributing to the needs of the Christian Jews who are needy and living in Jerusalem (Rom 15:25-26; 1 Cor 16:1; 2 Cor 8:4; 9:1).

Again, the early Christian congregations did *not* see themselves as a new religion, but as those who had received a new insight into the way God was at work to redeem all creation. Most traditional interpreters of Paul have written as though Christianity was inaugurated as a new religion immediately following the resurrection of Jesus, if not before. They have argued that just as Judaism saw itself as the sole possessor of truth and salvation, so Christianity as the "new Israel" was now the sole possessor of truth and salvation. But Paul never used the concept of the "new Israel." Rather, in Christ the promises of God are made available to non-Jews on the same basis as in Judaism at its best—faith in God alone.

An illustration of the kind of situation Paul possibly faced in Rome comes from Luke's Acts. In the sixth chapter he tells of an early argument in the Christian Jewish community between the Hebrew-speaking and the Greek-speaking Christian Jews. Stephen, one of the first Christian martyrs, plays a significant role in Paul's new insight into the will of God and consequently in the changing direction of his ministry. Stephen was a Greek-speaking Christian Jew. What is the issue in this argument between these Christian Jews? A.E. Harvey writes that

Jewish families who had lived for any length of time abroad had lost the habit of speaking either Aramaic or the sacred language of Hebrew, and had adopted Greek as their language. When such people returned to Jerusalem they continued to speak Greek, not only in secular life, but also in prayer and worship; they used a Greek translation of the Scriptures and attended a synagogue where the service was in Greek.[3]

However, the problem went much deeper than just language.

With the Greek language went a culture and a habit of thought very different from that of the Old Testament; and the Jews of the Dispersion, though they remained loyally and self-consciously Jewish, inevitably came to understand their ancestral faith in terms somewhat different from those still used by their kinsmen in Palestine.[4]

In particular, exposure to Greek philosophical approaches to religious expression may have caused them to see

the continual slaughter of animals which took place before the Temple in Jerusalem, and the emphasis on ritual and ceremonial matters which was characteristic of Palestinian Judaism, difficult to reconcile with the much more ethical and philosophical faith in which they had been brought up.[5]

Once the openness of the Christian message began to draw constituents from both traditional Jews and Greek Jews, it was only a matter of time before their differences would drive a wedge between them. And Luke says that the wedge became the very practical issue of the Greek-speaking widows being omitted in the daily distribution of food and aid. Stephen, along with the others, broke from that particular synagogue and set up their own form of organization for visitation and distribution.

Another theme that is introduced in these first verses is the distinction that Paul makes between Jesus the man and Christ the function. Paul tells us that Jesus is our brother in the faith and not equal to God, which would have been blasphemy. The Christ function springs from the divinity of God and works through particular persons. Listen to Paul here: "and when all things are thus subjected to God, then the Son himself will also be made subordinate to God who made all things subject to the Christ, and thus God will be all in all" (1 Cor 15:28). And here in Romans, he makes the distinction between the human Jesus and the exalted Christ in these words (1:3–4):

NEB	*RSV*
"on the human level he (Jesus) was *born of David's stock*, but on the level of the Spirit — the Holy Spirit — he was *declared* Son of God by a mighty act in that he rose from the dead."	"who was *descended* from David according to the flesh, and *designated* Son of God according to the Spirit of holiness by his resurrection from the dead."

Humanly speaking, Jesus was born as all of us were born, of human parents, but, as the NEB footnote informs us, was declared — designated, called, chosen, set apart — as Son of God *after* his resurrection. Paul does not talk of a pre-existent Jesus or a literal Son of God coming from heaven, but a very human man who was called by God and later raised by the power of God from the dead and then *designated* as a Son. Jesus became an heir of all that was God's — and we, his brothers and sisters, are fellow heirs. As Paul affirms in the eighth chapter:

> The Spirit you have received is ... a Spirit that makes us sons [and daughters], enabling us to cry "Abba! Father!" In that cry the Spirit of God joins with our spirits in testifying that we are God's children; and if children, then heirs. We are God's heirs and Christ's fellow-heirs, if we share his sufferings now in order to share his splendour hereafter.

3

The Collection for Jerusalem

It has been said somewhere that one of our basic difficulties with the study of Romans for our day is that "it deals with a Jewish/Christian conflict that is not a part of our situation today." The situation may be different, but the basic issues are the same. While the eating of food sacrificed to idols is not a contemporary issue in its literal form, the principle on which that issue rests is highly relevant to our situation.

Dr. William Farmer takes up this issue in an article, "The Dynamics of Christianity." When faced with the fundamental question of what we know with the greatest certainty about Jesus, Farmer agrees with Käsemann's reply: "he ate with sinners." The profundity of this statement is hidden in its overt simplicity. Farmer goes on to say that this fact is the basis on which we can realize the development between Jesus and Paul. Paul, too, must deal with the matter of eating with Gentiles. (It should be noted that "gentile" and "sinner" are often equated in the literature surrounding the beginning of the common era.) Christian Jews, under the leadership of Peter and James, had refused to eat with the uncircumcised Gentile Christians, although both Peter and James later changed on this matter. For both Jesus and Paul, the issue becomes centered in the theme of "self-righteous self-deception," i.e., thinking more highly of oneself than one ought. Thus, writes Farmer:

> If a tax collector can stand in the Temple and pray, "God be merciful to me a sinner," and then go down to his house justified before God, apart from the works of the law, then a "sinner out of Gentile origins" can do the same. He need only meet the conditions of a justifying faith, i.e., a faith based upon the

righteousness of God and not upon the works of the law (Rom 3:21-31).[1]

That which is the basis for Paul's gospel is one's relation to God's righteousness — a righteousness based not on works of law, but on self-giving love. And the way we know this is through the example of Jesus, "who was *descended* from David according to the flesh and *designated* Son of God in power according to the Spirit of holiness by his resurrection from the dead" (1:3-4). This Jesus, Paul proclaimed, not only called others to obedience of faith, but gave himself for our sins (5:6-8). By his life, death, and resurrection we have been called to be reconciled to God and to one another. All alike have sinned; in Christ all alike shall receive new life.

If Luke's account in his Acts is reliable, Paul came to this point of view over a period of time. Not long after he began preaching with the Christian Jews and Gentile Christians, the Jerusalem Conference was called over the matter of circumcision. While Paul seems to have won the debate, the compromise reached was that Gentile Christians should follow the law of Noah: they were to "abstain from what has been sacrificed to idols and from blood and from what is strangled and from unchastity" (Acts 15:29). Unchastity here refers to the pagan temple prostitution. Paul agreed to these conditions, and as he tells us in Galatians, he agreed to make a collection for the poor Christian Jews in Jerusalem as a sign of his good faith.

Luke pressed his point of Paul's complete dedication to the unity of Christian Jews and other Christians by going ahead, after winning the fight at the Jerusalem Conference, and circumcising Timothy (16:3). Paul and Silas were accused of being "Jews who advocate customs which it is not lawful for us Romans to accept or practice" (16:21). Paul observed the Jewish rituals concerning vows (18:18), and therefore had his hair cut off after leaving Corinth.

What was the significance of Paul's "haircut"? Solemnly cutting off one's hair was a custom deriving from Numbers 6, in which a man publicly announced a vow to keep himself ritually clean, to abstain from wine, and to allow his hair to grow again until the vow was completed, at which time it would be cut again. Practically, it was a public vow made to strengthen one's commitment to the vow. At the end of the period the man would present his cut-off hair as a part of his offering in the Temple.

As mentioned earlier, Luke was very concerned that Paul's

relationship to Judaism be kept intact. Perhaps this vow had related to Paul's early promise to take his gospel to Jews first. If so, the ending of the vow might be indicated in Acts 18:6 as Paul completed his preaching in Corinth: "And when they opposed and reviled him, Paul shook out his garments and said to them, 'Your blood be upon yours heads! I am innocent! From now on I will go to the Gentiles'!" However, I believe it to be more likely that the completion of the vow signified that the collection had been safely delivered to the officials of the congregations in Jerusalem.

Luke is eager to maintain Paul's image of commitment to the Christian Jews, and therefore has Paul submit to the Jewish rituals of purification upon arrival in Jerusalem (21:17–26). Paul must, and does according to Luke, proclaim that Christian Jews are not required to abandon Moses and Jewish custom. In fact, Paul proclaims his oneness with the Christian Jews in Jerusalem, saying: "I am a Pharisee, a son of Pharisees; with respect to the hope and the resurrection of the dead I am on trial" (23:6). And rather than seeing his old life before his Road-to-Damascus experience as being a sinful state, he boasts: "I have lived before God in all good conscience up to this day!" The only sin Paul speaks of is his persecution of the new Christian sect. His conversion was less a change of religion than a change in direction within the same religion. Paul sees his following of the Way as a part of Judaism. It is his detractors who claim that he is abandoning the religion of his heritage. In Caesarea, in the courtroom of the governor Felix, Paul confirms his stance:

> But this I admit to you, that according to the Way, *which they call a sect*, I worship the God of our fathers, believing everything laid down by the law or written in the prophets, having a hope in God *which these themselves accept*, that there will be a resurrection of both the just and the unjust. So I always take pains to have a clear conscience toward God and men. Now after some years I came to bring *my nation* alms and offerings (Acts 24:14–17).

And the Pharisees there defend Paul with these words: "We find nothing wrong in this man. What if a spirit or an angel spoke to him?" (23:9).

Paul's mission to the Gentiles was to bring them the message of justification and reconciliation in a way previously undeveloped and in large part thought to be unavailable to them. Paul's vision of the Christ convinced him that if God was truly God and Creator of all the people, and being one God as Moses had taught in the Decalogue, then the salvation God was offering in Jesus must also be to all the people. And if it is for all people, then Jesus' action in eating with sinners and Paul's preaching to Gentiles were entirely consistent. As God said to Peter in a vision: "What God has proclaimed clean, you must not call unclean" (Acts 10:15).

Paul's return to Jerusalem completed his vow and made his word firm concerning the faithfulness of Gentile Christians. The vow was the collection for Jerusalem's poor Christian Jews (Rom 15:26). The major reason Paul gives for making this collection a test of faithfulness to the Christian Jews is: "for if the Gentiles have come to share in their blessings, they ought also to be of service to them in material blessings" (Rom 15:27). The success of this collection, which we generally read over or take for granted, would determine the unity of the early Christian congregations. Paul had made a vow to the Jerusalem Conference, and he could not continue his mission to Spain and Rome until that vow was fulfilled. This task was worth the cost of his very life, for he knew that going to Jerusalem might mean either imprisonment or death — or both.

4

What Is Salvation?

While meditating on Romans 1:16–17, Martin Luther suddenly grasped the insight that the righteousness of God – God's righting action – was not to be found in God's retributive justice or rewards and punishments but rather in divine mercy and grace which is available to all. This was not, of course, new to Paul or to the Christian sect. Nor did it come to Martin Luther without considerable background pushing him in that direction. Neither is this foreign to the thought of Judaism, either of the years surrounding the beginning of the common era or of our present day. As Jewish philosopher Elliot N. Dorff has written: "God is just. That is, despite the evidence of the Holocaust, I still believe that justice, morality, and compassion are crucial, even if they are not rewarded."[1] This is quite familiar to the faith affirmed by the prophet Habakkuk (3:17–18). Dorff goes on:

> I agree that it is *easier* to be motivated to observe the commandments if you think that God will punish you for not observing them and reward you if you do; but, as the Rabbis recognized elsewhere, (a) that is *not* the proper motivation (*Avot* 1:3); (b) it does not even work out that way, at least as far as we know, and it must, therefore, eventually lose force as a motivation; and (c) moreover, it *is* possible to observe Jewish law without a theological whipping stick – indeed, without God at all.[2]

In the end, he declares, "the only reward for performing a *mizvah* is having done it and the impetus which that gives to performing another *mizvah*."[3]

39

A humorous and yet insightful account of *mizvah* or mitzvah comes from Dave Berg in his book, *My Friend God*. He tells how Moses Maimonides in the twelfth century established eight stages of mitzvah, each higher than the next:

> The highest degree is to make the man who needs charity *self-supporting*. The next highest degree is where the one that *gives* and the one that *receives* are *not* aware of each other. The third inferior degree is where the *recipient* knows the *giver*, but the giver does *not* know the recipient. The fifth degree is where the giver puts alms into the hands of the poor *without being asked*. The sixth degree is where he puts money into the hands of the poor *after* being asked. The seventh degree is where he gives *less* than he should, but does so *cheerfully*. The eighth degree is where he gives *resentfully*.[4]

The catch to all of this, says Berg, is that when you do a good deed you cannot tell anyone. Otherwise, it is not a good deed but a selfish deed. Now, writes Berg, "By telling you how to earn a *mitzvah*, I have *earned a mitzvah*. But by telling, I could lose it. Since you didn't read this paragraph, you don't know I told, and *I didn't lose it!*"[5]

Let us look at 1:16–17 in its various translations and the *Living Bible* paraphrase:

KJV	*RSV*
For I am not ashamed of the gospel of Christ: for it is the power of God unto salvation to everyone that believeth; to the Jew first, and also to the Greek. For therein is the righteousness of God revealed from faith to faith: as it is written, the just shall live by faith.	For I am not ashamed of the gospel: it is the power of God for salvation to every one who has faith, to the Jew first and also to the Greek. For in it the righteousness of God is revealed through faith for faith; as it is written, "He who through faith is righteous shall live."

JerB

For I am not ashamed of the Good News: it is the power of God saving all who have faith — Jews first, but Greeks as well — since this is what reveals the justice of God to us: it shows how faith leads to faith, or as scripture says: "The upright man finds life through faith."

NEB

For I am not ashamed of the Gospel. It is the saving power of God for everyone who has faith — the Jew first, but the Greek also — because here is revealed God's way of righting wrong,* a way that starts from faith and ends in faith: as Scripture says, "he shall gain life who is justified through faith."

It is based on faith and addressed to faith.

TEV

For I have complete confidence in the gospel: it is God's power to save all who believe, first the Jews and also the Gentiles. For the gospel reveals how God puts men right with himself: it is through faith alone, from beginning to end. As the scripture says, "He who is put right with God through faith shall live."

Phillips

For I am not ashamed of the gospel. I see it as the very power of God working for the salvation of everyone who believes it, both Jew and Greek. I see in it God's plan for imparting righteousness to men, a process begun and continued by their faith. For, as the scripture says: The righteous shall live by faith.

Living Bible

For I am not ashamed of this Good News about Christ. It is God's powerful method of bringing all who believe it to heaven. This message was preached first to the Jews alone, but now everyone is invited to come to God in this same way. This Good News tells us that God makes us ready for heaven — makes us right in God's sight — when we put our faith and trust in Christ to save us. This is accomplished from start to finish by faith. As the Scripture says it, "the man who finds life will find it through trusting God."

These two verses raise essential questions concerning our christology, the meaning of salvation, and the meaning of related concepts.

"I am not ashamed of the *gospel*." Is the "gospel" the promise of heaven, as Taylor insists in his paraphrase? None of the translations even remotely suggest a connection of the two terms. And nowhere in Romans does Paul even make such an implication. Rather, the gospel is the good news of God's faithfulness to *all* people of faith. And the promise of the gospel is much more than the individualism implied by Taylor. In each letter, Paul talks of the promise as being the uniting of all creation in God's eternal life. It appears that Taylor has taken extreme liberties in his paraphrase.

We shall be led astray if we limit this term "gospel" to only the New Testament aspect of it. Paul plainly states that the good news was part of the Jewish heritage. The term is found in several instances in the Old Testament and in the intertestamental writings. It refers to the good news of God's loving care and his faithfulness to his promises. Here in verses 16–17 the gospel refers to the *Gospel of God*, one of Paul's most frequently used phrases. Again, our christology gets in the way of our theology, and Taylor represents a particular abuse of this since many accept his paraphrase as holy writ. Gospel – Good News! – this gives us the image of a runner hastening on to the next town with a message from the king that is vitally important to the whole community. It is a public announcement. Everyone alike participates in it, and its reception issues in a joyful response.

What, then, is salvation? It is not clearly defined, probably because Paul assumed that his readers have already made some sort of faith commitment and are therefore well aware of what it means. And, like the term gospel, salvation means various things depending on the person's situation when it is experienced. But having said that, we may state a general principle concerning salvation: salvation is responding in complete trust that God will do what God has promised to do. It is relying on God's presence, care and loving guidance – *even when outward circumstances and inward experience may not confirm these things*.

Sobrino[6] discusses the "crisis of Galilee" for Jesus, and tells us that after this crucial point Jesus' confidence in God's kingdom is a "hope against hope." Letting God remain God now lacked verification for Jesus. When we see Jesus hanging on the cross, we see a man abandoned even by God, at least in his experience. The joy of *experiencing* God's leading and comfort are absent. And we hear him cry out: "My God, my God, why have you abandoned me?" Yet he could also say, "Father, into your hands I commend my spirit."

Salvation means no longer being a slave to the destructive powers in life. It means that sin is no more the controlling factor. It does not mean that one will no longer sin, but that sin is no longer in control of one's motives and behavior patterns.

This might be best illustrated from a common life experience arising in the mother/married daughter relationship. After the daughter has married and established her own home, the mother still tries to control the behavior and decisions of the daughter. The daughter often gives in under the pressure or simply because it is easier to live that way. Somehow the apron strings have never been severed. After a while, though, the daughter throws up her hands in desperation. She still loves her mother, but she cries out: "I wish mother would quit trying to run my life!" Who has the primary decision here? The daughter, obviously. She simply has not exercised, or had the power to exercise, that decision-making option. She cannot control the behavior of her mother, but through the grace and support of others, she can make the decision to control her own.

Or a man carried throughout his life an anger against another, or perhaps several others. Especially in a smaller community where everyone knows what you are doing, and with or to whom, the problem may become acute and someone cries out: "I wish something would happen to change that man!" Or, "I wish that man would move as far away from me as possible!" Or, "I wish he would do something about his offensive behavior!" As obnoxious as this person may be, where does the real decision lie? Can I, by wishing, change the other person? Does the other person really *make* me angry, or is the anger my decision? The decision to become angry is my decision to make. And it is my decision to either allow or not allow his offensive behavior to control me. The other man must decide for himself that he no longer wishes to live in his self-imposed hell.

The gospel message of salvation, then, says that there is a way out of life's dilemmas. There is a power that can come to us from God which will enable us to throw off the shackles of slavery and bondage. It does not mean for the daughter that mother will stop trying to manipulate her life or her home; nor does it mean that the obnoxious man will no longer be a thorn in the flesh. But it does mean that we can have the power to deal with the matter in an open and creative way, in a manner that the manipulation and anger does not destroy us. Just as the power of God did not prevent the crucifixion, it did provide a way for life to defeat the powers of death.

Salvation: saved from the power of sin, estrangement, and enslavement to baser desires. This is the message of salvation. Sin will remain in the world, but it need not control us. It means that through God we now can have the power to decide whether evil impulses will control us or whether we will control them.

And that is a tremendous power. It is said that 80 percent of all persons in doctors' offices are there from illnesses which are self-imposed or self-created. The power of salvation says that we do not have to use that kind of a crutch anymore. We can face life and be victorious.

Of course, salvation is much more than that. It is the proclamation of the Kingdom of God in this world which demands changed social structures. It means an open and accepting way of living and being in community. And ultimately, it means that the whole of the created universe will be caught up in the eternal life of God. Salvation, the inflowing power of God, makes life truly life and results in a faith relationship with God that is so intimate that nothing—not even death—can destroy it. Salvation is to base your total life in the belief that "in everything God works for good with those who love him, who are called according to his purposes" (8:28).

Such a faith is born from faith—from the faithfulness of God. From faith we go on to even stronger faith until that relationship with God is the source, guide, and goal of our existence.

5

Has God Abandoned the Jews?

The letter to the Romans answers a question crucial to both Jew and Gentile, both Jew and Christian: *Has God abandoned the Jews?* And the even larger question: *Is God faithful or capricious?* For Jews, the question arose over the fact that Gentiles were responding to the new tradition of Jesus. Since they were responding to the word that God's promises are to all without distinction, Jews wondered: Has God now abandoned us as a mistake or a failure? And further, what of the promises to Abraham, Moses, and the other ancestors: Are these vain promises and now invalidated? Do we now hold a hope without hope?

For Gentile Christians the questions were no easier. After the initial glow, the hard intellectual work of developing the implications of this new relationship began, and they asked much the same question as did the Jews: What assurance do Gentiles have that God will not change the promises now extended to them? If in making this extension God has abandoned the divine assurance given to Jews, then the same might happen to Gentile Christians. If salvation through the faith exhibited in Abraham can be taken from Jews, then salvation through the faith exemplified in Jesus can be taken from Gentile Christians. Thus, the same basic question plagued both Christian Jews and Gentile Christians: Is God faithful? Or, is God fickle (like the Roman gods)? Is the divine love trustworthy, or is it inconstant?

Paul's firm and unswerving answer was that God is faithful, and this faithfulness is guaranteed to all who have faith in God—Jew and Gentile alike! The faithfulness of God is reliable. Therefore, there is no discontinuity between the faith of Abraham and the faith of Jesus. The focus of both is God. Out of the promises to

45

the ancestors and prophets grew this present reality of the inclusion of Gentiles. Thus, the "righteousness of God is revealed through faith for faith." The faithfulness of God is the basis for our faith. Such righteousness refers to God's loving kindness, God's steadfast love (*chesedh* or *hesed*). Paul declared that the steadfast love of God can be trusted to save all who have faith. This means that God will be loyal to the divine promises made to Abraham that the people of many nations, "a multitude of nations," would be included in the covenant, i.e., that Yahweh would "be God to you and your descendants after you" (Gen 17:7). Just as God promised the people through the prophet Jeremiah, "I have loved you with an everlasting love; therefore I have continued my faithfulness to you" (3:3), so now God offers this steadfast love and faithfulness to all persons through the witness of Jesus Christ: "the righteousness of God is revealed through faith for faith." We therefore, Jew and non-Jew alike, may feel secure in the guidance of God.

The steadfast love and faithfulness of God is a constant theme in Jewish scripture and literature. God is seen as making vows with a chosen people, vows which are lasting, continual, firm, permanent, and sure. This faithfulness is the foundation and source of human faith. It is a loving kindness on which one can rely. It gives assurance for an unknown and unknowable future. *Hesed* is therefore a value judgment ascribed to God from experience. And Christians today can make that judgment only from God's faithfulness to the descendants of Abraham.

Paul declares that the righteousness of God is available to *all* who have faith in God. Jews received this first through the witness of Abraham, but it is now realized that it is available to all. This is consistent with the Old Testament revelation of the priority of faith. As Jespen writes: "Since God is *'el 'emeth* (a faithful God), man's relationship to this God is possible only through *'emeth,*" that is, honestly, genuinely, reliably.[1] One must speak honestly, from the depth of one's being. Therefore, the Psalmist relied not on deeds but on faith and trust in God's *hesed*: "But I have trusted in thy steadfast love; my heart shall rejoice in thy salvation" (13:5); "Many are the pangs of the wicked; but steadfast love surrounds him who trusts in the Lord" (32:10). And the entire 136th Psalm is built around the theme of God's faithfulness. The prophet Jeremiah spoke of the loving kindness of God as well as our human response in faith to that love:

> Thus says the Lord: "Let not the wise man glory in his wisdom, let not the mighty man glory in his might, let not the rich man glory in his riches; *but let him who glories glory in this,* that he understands and knows me, that I am the Lord who practices steadfast love, justice, and righteousness in the earth; for in these things I delight, says the Lord" (9:23–24).

Righteousness, then, is to be understood in light on this steadfast love. It is not so much an act of fulfilling laws or customs, although that may be our response to it, but righteousness is that which stems from the very motivation for all of life: faithfulness and promise.

Literally, righteousness means putting things right, which in turn implies a divine purposefulness. In this way, Paul sees the righteousness of God not in legal terms, but in the sense of vindicating or justifying love. Krister Stendahl points out that the righteousness of God for Paul is not described as redeeming some and condemning others. It does not say that everyone will be saved, nor does it say that some will be saved and others damned. Paul is confident that God alone can make such a determination. However, he agrees with his Hebrew heritage in saying that there are two basic impulses striving within each person: the good impulse, *yetser tob,* and the evil impulse, *yetser ha-ra'.* The righteousness of God puts things right within by defeating the power of evil impulses which rule our lives.

Later we shall see how Paul speaks of this righteousness on a more social and cosmic level. He does not negate the personal character of God's righteousness, but he states that any personal salvation is also part of a much larger perspective. This destroys the notion of individualism and exclusivism, both of which are forms of idolatry whereby we single ourselves out as the *only* really important item on life's agenda.

To see the theme of righteousness in relationship to steadfast love, as well as in relation to Paul's later theme of "oneness in Christ," we need to see the Hebrew references to righteousness. There we find that an act is evil, not because it breaks the law, but because it breaks a community relationship of covenant. The purpose of being a covenant people was to preserve the notion of the personal in community. Consequently, righteousness was that which preserved or restored this sense of community, this oneness in the purpose of God. The righteousness of God, although revealed first to the Jews, is now also revealed through Jesus Christ to the Gentiles as that which creates a new community in which all people are to be equally included as members. Creation is to be renewed in its essential oneness. Therefore Paul can refer to Christ as the Second Adam, the new creation, the one body representing the various and differing members, etc. It is because of this righting action of God, creating a new or renewed sense of the community of all through a circumcision of the heart, that Paul finds his vocation to preach the Gospel of God to the Gentiles. Thus, the righting action of God deals with the critical question of whether and how Gentiles are included in God's people, in the covenant community.

We have tried to demonstrate in earlier parts of this study that this Christian emphasis on bringing Gentiles into the covenant community was not new to either Jesus or Paul. Both were a part of their times, and their times are to be seen in the context of the great amount of missionary activity, or proselyting, going on in Judaism. We are prone to believe — indeed, we have been led to believe — that the decades surrounding the first century of the common era were times of deadness for Judaism. We are well aware that Judaism was called to be God's witness among the peoples of the earth and a light to all the nations. But we have been led to believe that Judaism failed in that calling. Therefore, we are somewhat surprised to discover that "Jewish religious tradition found its crystallization in the Pharisaic-rabbinic period, and one of its active concerns was to wage an active campaign to disseminate its teachings throughout the pagan world."[2] While welcoming converts with a special love, conversion was not the main objective of this Jewish campaign. Rabbi Bokser explains that conversion demands an absolutized system of rite and ritual, so that the witness seeks "to alienate a person from his own faith ." But, he writes:

> Judaism never defined its own system of rite and doctrine in such terms. It did not absolutize them, and, therefore, did not seek to universalize them. It regarded them as channels of a transcendent light, as vessels containing a truth which resides in them and is cultivated through them, but that truth has a life of its own that is capable of reaching and enriching other lives outside its own system. Only the truth expressed is universal and needs to be diffused through the act of witness, and this truth can enrich other lives regardless of any formal affiliation with any particular religious system.[3]

Indeed, says Bokser,

> in some cases, Jewish missionaries sought to dissuade a would-be convert from formal initiation into Judaism. They counselled him, instead, to remain in his own household of faith but to live by the new light of the Jewish principles which transcended the formalized in its rites and ceremonies.[4]

Salvation, then, is based on faith in the righteous revelation of God's own faithfulness. As a famous Rabbi of the twelfth century wrote: "You must realize that the Torah seeks the heart, and everything depends on the intentions of the heart."[5]

In his book *Jesus' Promise to the Nations*, Jeremias argues that Jewish hope did not exclude the salvation of the Gentiles. In the end, after appropriate purification has occurred, the whole world will come under God's rule. We hear Paul saying this to the congregations in Corinth: "When all things are subjected to God, then the Son himself will also be subjected to God who put all things under him, that God may be everything to everyone" (1 Cor 15:28; Eph 1:10). Jeremias writes: "With this in mind, the Jews, and especially the scribes and Pharisees, were already busy with a massive missionary activity."[6] He also gives evidence that "Jesus came upon the scene in the midst of what was *par excellence* the missionary age of Jewish history."[7]

Paul, then, as we argued in the introduction, is to be seen as a Jewish missionary, called by God to bring the light of divine steadfast love to the Gentiles that through the witness of Jesus Christ they, too, might know this faithfulness of God and the promises of Israel. Paul became convinced that the life, death, and resurrection of Jesus Christ was God's revelation that the good news of freedom from the impulses of evil was available to *all* persons, so that from that time on, there would be no distinctions made between persons in terms of superiority or chosenness. Therefore he writes: "There is neither Jew nor Greek, there is neither slave nor free, there is neither male nor female; for you are all one in Christ Jesus!" (Gal 3:28; Rom 10:12)

As a Christian Jewish missionary, Paul's main concern was to clarify how Gentiles are now heirs to the promises of Abraham: "And if you are Christ's, *then you are Abraham's offspring*, heirs according to promise" (Gal 3:29). Thus, Christian Gentiles become in a sense honorary Jews by God's grace as declared in the witness of Jesus Christ. There is, then, a limit to Paul's missionary urge in terms of conversion to some new religion outside of or apart from Judaism.

Therefore, we live from faith, through faith, and to faith — our faith originates in the faithfulness of God, and continues to draw strength from that faith handed on to us from God's various channels of revelation. It is also instructive to note that Paul carries on the rabbinic tradition in his usage of Habakkuk 2:4. The rabbis saw this verse as a "comprehensive fulfilment of the commandments in meritorious faithfulness."[8]

John Calvin commented on Romans 1:17 where Paul quotes the prophet Habakkuk and reminds us that Paul, in his proof-texting method, forgets to add the very important first part of Habakkuk's verse: "Behold, he whose soul is not upright in him shall fail." This has been interpreted, Calvin wrote, as: "whoever is proud and thinks himself well-fortified will always have a troubled mind." These persons torment themselves. They decide one thing, but prefer another. It is then that the prophet declared: "*but* the righteous (or just) shall live by faith." Thus, Calvin continued:

> I have no doubt that the prophet here sets faith over against all the safeguards with which men blind themselves in order to neglect God himself and to avoid asking aid from him. Because men put themselves in subjection to earthly things, and rely upon the falsehoods in which they trust, the prophet here ties life to faith. But faith...depends upon God alone. Therefore, "to live by faith" means to abandon voluntarily all the defenses which so often fail us. One who knows himself destitute of all protection will live in his faith if he seeks whatever he needs from God alone....[9]

Calvin was convinced that all persons desire to make themselves secure. But the person of faith knows that life and its meaning come from God alone. Thus, Paul can write that faith issues from faith — our faithfulness is born of God's own faithfulness. It is through faith that both Jews and Christians, and indeed, all persons, are able to proceed in faith and thereby be unified with God, with one another, and with oneself.

6

Idolatry

A.E. Harvey has written that it is probably safe to say that the years surrounding the beginning of the common era were filled with the belief "that the prevailing immorality of contemporary society was connected with the rejection of pure religion. The existence of God was axiomatic" or self-evident.[1] Paul certainly agreed with this as he charged that "the wrath of God is revealed from heaven against all ungodliness and wickedness of men who by their wickedness suppress the truth" of God's existence (1:18–23). This ungodliness may refer to a general lack of respect for monotheistic religion in the Greco-Roman world, while wickedness clearly refers to the suppression or outright hostility toward religious and moral endeavors. Paul points to God as the Author and God of all existence, and says that, if for no other reason, we can see the attributes of God through our rational faculties. Therefore there is evil in the world, both personal and collective, because persons and society have rejected this truth of God which is everywhere evident. As William Baird has written: "Bad theology means bad ethics." The confusion between the creation and creator "leads to chaos in the moral arena."[2]

The consequences of this rejection must run their course. Indeed, the message of Paul here relates to our own moral life. As H.R. Niebuhr pointed out several years ago, our problem may be that we have too many gods. We, too, must deal with the consequences of our polytheism and idolatry. And this Paul refers to as the "wrath of God," or the "judgment of God." This judgment is not only at the end of history but is already present in the conditions of life, and these Paul lists. Robinson quotes Dodd's recognition of the dual nature of "wrath" (orgē):

Paul never says that God is angry, as he says that God is loving and gracious. In fact only here and in Col 3.6 = Eph 5.6 is it specifically the wrath of God.... "Wrath" is the process of inevitable retribution which comes into operation when God's laws are broken.[3]

Wrath, then, deals with the inevitable result of sin. As Robinson points out, it is an *effectus* or effect, not an *affectus* or emotion. It is therefore "essentially the perversion of a *personal* relationship." Wrath is not a "capricious of irrational rage" on the part of God, but "a deeply personal abhorrence, such as love must always feel in the presence of injustice or cruelty."[4]

Since wrath is understood in terms of its relationship to the loving character of God, we are forced to realize that when God "hands over" (1:18) the sinner, God does not abandon the sinner to anything outside the divine sphere. As Robinson writes:

> it does not express [God's] emotion; but it does express his responsibility.... The revelation of [God's] righteousness and his wrath are in fact one and the same revelation. Indeed, it is this inalienable personal quality of wrath, even as wrath, the fact that we cannot sin ourselves out of the structure of our being as persons in personal relationship with God, which is the *saving* factor in our otherwise desperate situation.[5]

Thus, for God to hand over the sinners to their own desires does not mean that their unfaithfulness has made God unfaithful. It means that the immoral or estranged condition of human life has forced God's love to be experienced as wrath. In this way even sin cooperates to promote the glory of God. "What sin does is to transform man's inescapable personal relationship to God from a relationship which feels like being at home to a relationship which feels like being in prison."[6]

Paul looks around him and sees moral decadence, idolatry, and the dehumanization of the human passion through prostitution, homosexuality, venereal disease ("paid in their own persons the fitting wage of such perversion"), as well as various kinds of ungracious behavior. Because of their rejection of the truth of God's revelations the people are filled with injustice, covetousness, and mischief; they are consumed with evil thoughts of envy, murder, rivalry and treachery; they are gossips, arrogant, boastful, and haters of God; they show no loyalty to God or to family, and are inventors of all kinds of new evils; they have no conscience and are not faithful to their word; they are heartless (without natural affections) and ruthless (without pity).

All of this can be summed up under the one basic heading of *idolatry*, the elevation and worship of anything or anyone that is not God. It is to make something finite into an ultimate. It is making a god out of anything other than God—whether it is the state, a system of politics or government, a leader, another person, or even oneself. The prophets wrote that any act can be idolatrous since idolatry arises out of the intentions of one's heart. Jeremiah chides: "My people have committed two evils: they have forsaken me, the fountain of living water, and hewed out cisterns for themselves, broken cisterns, that can hold no water" (2:13). A partial list of things considered by the prophets as idolatrous would include the following:

Pride in one's own wisdom (thinking oneself smarter than God)

Trust in beauty (the vanity of conceit)

Self-sufficiency (not needing God)

Reliance on horses and chariots (trust in military might)

Trust in foreign alliances (selling one's values for false security)

Claims of personal innocence (blaming others for one's sins)

Being too secure (denial for need of God; sense of false security)

Immunity to God's demands (God is talking to someone else!)

Immunity to God's vision (living in a hopeless past)

Denial of the reality of God (making a god of one's own system of reality)

Lying (denial of truth; since God is truth, a denial of God)

Indifference to the fatherless, widows, and needy (self-centeredness)

Gaining wealth by immoral means (making a god of self)

Thus, to seek one's own purposes and individual security at the expense of others was considered idolatrous since it denied community and through its individualism made oneself a god. It is based on a false sense of security which urges one's own interest and the seeking of advantage over others.

Idolatry also destroys the hiddenness of God which is basic to biblical monotheism. The hiddenness of God can be seen in the struggle between the hill shrines and the Temple in Jerusalem. When too much emphasis was placed on one, the prophets sought a balance by preaching in favor of the other. Minear speaks to the importance of this: "The very hiddenness of God marks his superiority to idols. It is his hiddenness that requires that men must seek him with their whole heart. They must seek him in a different way from that in which they seek an idol."[7]

When we remember that section II of this letter (1:18–4:15) is addressed to the "weak in faith" who rely heavily upon the law and enjoy judging others in terms of it, it is necessary that we see 1:20b and 2:1 together. It might appear that Paul is setting them up for a fall. He begins by agreeing with them that the godless and wicked Gentiles have no excuse for their sin, nor for the wrath with which they are being judged. These weak in faith must have felt very good and even more superior to the evil Gentiles. But then suddenly Paul turns the spotlight on them with these words: "THEREFORE, *you* have no excuse, O man, whoever you are, when you judge another; for in passing judgment upon him you condemn yourself, because you, the judge, are doing the very same thing!"

And what is it they are doing? In judging others they have committed idolatry by setting themselves up as God over the life of other human beings. In forcing their belief and their way of life onto someone else as *the only way*, they made themselves as God over them. And that, says scripture in all parts, is idolatry, and in fact, destroys the cornerstone of not only the Mosaic Law but the intent of creation as well.

Now, says Paul, if the Gentiles who are not under the Mosaic Law will be judged because of their idolatry, will not those who are under the law be more severely judged. Or, asks Paul, "do you presume upon the riches of God's kindness and forbearance and patience? Do you suppose that you will escape the judgment of God. Are you trying to take advantage of God?"

In 2:8 Paul again points to idolatry, this time to "those who are factious"—those governed by selfish ambition, who cause dissention and thereby destroy the basis of community. It is not just Gentiles outside the law who are idolatrous. All alike are guilty, both Jew and non-Jew. Therefore, "God shows no partiality in his judgments" (2:11). Moses taught the same thing: "For the Lord your God is God of gods and Lord of lords, the great, the mighty, and the terrible God *who is not partial* and takes no bribe" (Dt 10:17).

Or, as the NEB translates Paul's words: "He is no respector of persons." God's only criterion is the extent to which one carries out the intent of the divine word, both as it is written in scripture and on the heart. Thus, says Paul, "if you have not known the law, you will not be judged by the law. But if you have known the law and sinned, you will be judged by it." However, in the final analysis, such distinctions are no escape, since "it is not the *hearers* of the law who are righteous before God, but the *doers* of the law who will be justified" (2:13).[8] Paul is clear in saying that although one does not know the law (and perhaps to be consistent, Jesus Christ?) yet does what is right, "their conscience is called as witness, and their own thoughts argue the case on either side, against them or for them" (2:15). Having the law inscribed on the heart was also a theme of the prophet Jeremiah:

> The time is coming, says the Lord, when I will make a new covenant with Israel and Judah.... I will set my law within them and write it on their hearts; I will become their God and they shall become my people. No longer need they teach one another to know the Lord; all of them, high and low alike, shall know me, says the Lord, for I will forgive their wrongdoings and remember their sin no more (31:31–34).

And Moses had taught the same thing:

> For this commandment which I command you this day is not too hard for you, neither is it far off. It is not in heaven, that you should say, "who will go up for us to heaven, and bring it to us, that we may hear it and do it?" Neither is it beyond the sea, that you should say, "Who will go over the sea for us, and bring it to us, that we may hear it and do it?" But the word is very near you; it is in your mouth and in your heart, so that you can do it (Dt 30:11–14).

Those who do what is right before God are justified — and their hearts and consciences bear witness to the fact that they have entered a genuine covenant with God.

Those who judge others presume to put themselves above all others. They put themselves in the position of playing God with the lives of others. As God, they presume to declare who is and who is not worthy of being treated as a person formed in the image of

God. But in their judging they misuse others for their own purposes and, as such, destroy that divine image. Therefore, behind all sin is the ambition to be God, to have the power of control and manipulation over God's creation and God's creatures.

7

Of What Value Is Circumcision?

What is the value of circumcision (2:25–3:26)? Indeed, what is the value of baptism? The issue in this chapter revolves around the larger question of the faithfulness of God in relation to the external symbols of the community. Scripture holds that God had commanded Abraham and all his descendants to be circumcised (Gen 17:1–27). Had God now changed his mind and declared circumcision to be of no value? Is that which God once commanded now to be revoked? And if this be so, what about the other commands — nay, what about the promises? Will these, too, be changed or be made invalid? Again, is God fickle?

Christians have never been free from such questioning. Most of the ceremonies and rites observed by the Church were carried over from Judaism by the primitive communities which considered them still valid. Now then, asks the Christian, if the mind of God was changed concerning the command to be circumcised, is it not possible, indeed probable, that Christians will also find themselves cut off in the future?

Therefore, the question is important for the principle involved: What *is* the value of circumcision? For centuries this rite had functioned as a symbol of Jewish tribal and national unity, and later it developed into the sign of the covenant relationship which existed not only between the people, but also between the people and God. And as their conception of God developed, the symbol became important as a physical sign of unwavering devotion to the one God.

If Paul were to address Christians today, as he most certainly does in the words of scripture properly understood, he would pose the same sort of question: "What is the value of baptism? Or what

advantage is there in being a Christian?" Many Christians have the
same smug feeling that Paul encountered in his ministry. Many also
demand the outward sign as that which saves. It is not unusual to
hear the words from Christian pulpits, "You need only believe *and*
be baptized." Accepting the revelation of God in the witness of
Jesus Christ is apparently not enough for these Christians. Baptism
is absolutely necessary. Of course, scripture has never taught that
circumcision or baptism or prayers at the altar could save anyone,
even though when they are properly understood they may be effective channels for the grace of God. We need to keep this contemporary challenge before us as we study Paul's challenge to the Jews
and Gentiles in Rome.

It is often assumed by present-day Christians that the concept
of circumcision of the heart (2:29) originated with the coming of
Christ. However, more than 600 years *before* Christ the prophet
Jeremiah began interpreting circumcision as more than the physical
loss of genital foreskin. He spoke also of circumcising one's ears
and one's heart: "Circumcise yourselves to the Lord, remove the
foreskin of your hearts" (4:4); "Behold their ears are uncircumcised,
they cannot listen" (6:10); "Behold the days are coming, says the
Lord, when I will punish all those who are circumcised yet uncircumcised" (9:25); and, "all the house of Israel is uncircumcised in
heart" (9:26). Recording earlier thoughts and yet written down later
under the reign of Josiah, the books of Leviticus and Deuteronomy
speak of the circumcised heart: "if then their uncircumcised heart is
humbled and they make amends for their iniquity...." (Lev 26:41);
"Circumcise therefore the foreskin of your heart, and be no longer
stubborn" (Dt 10:16); and, "the Lord your God will circumcise your
heart and the hearts of your offsprings, so that you will love the
Lord your God with all your mind and with all your soul, that you
may live" (Dt 30:6). Like Jesus six centuries later, Jeremiah did not
deny the validity of physical circumcision as a sign of covenant,
nor could Paul when we consider his understanding of baptism.
(Paul obviously had as much trouble with baptism among these
new Christians as he had with circumcision among Christian Jews.
This led him to say to the congregations in Corinth, "I thank God
that I baptized none of you except..." [1 Cor 1:14].)

By the time of the Maccabees two centuries before the
common era, circumcision took on the meaning of an essential
national identity for which one was willing to die (1 Macc 1:60–64;
2 Macc 6:10; 4 Macc 4:25 – see page 20 above). Rudolf Meyer

writes that "the religious conflicts under Antiochus IV (176-163 B.C.E.) which were in the last resort caused by the attempts at reform made by certain circles in Jerusalem, led to the prohibition of circumcision."[1] Thus, many gave their lives to preserve this holy covenant which they had made with God. As could be expected, some did abandon the practice as they fled from Jerusalem. However, they took with them the idea that if the holy covenant was not to be further profaned, then some reinterpretation was necessary which would somehow include the intent of the practice without relying in external and permanent forms. Many found this reinterpretation in the prophetic writing, and their descendants welcomed Paul's stance which relied on Jeremiah.

For Palestinian Judaism the physical significance and meaning of circumcision grew and was made firm through 200 years of war, persecution, and foreign occupation. With such a background, it ought not surprise us that the rabbis rejected any attempt to redefine circumcision in spiritual terms alone. For them it had to be a both/and situation: it is *both* physical *and* spiritual. One could not be lost without destroying the other. Something purchased at so great a price could not be treated lightly. Therefore, in the years surrounding the beginning of the common era, circumcision was made a compulsory prerequisite for almost every social dealing. Persecution had been so severe that the idea of a messianic age in which there would be *no gentiles* became prevalent. This was an over-reaction, but an understandable one. Such was the environment of much of the early Christian movement.

Taking Jeremiah as his model, Paul put this question to his readers: *If* circumcision represents more than the loss of physical genital foreskin, is it not, then, the covenant to which it points that is the really important focus? Paul desired no more to destroy or profane the holy covenant than did those of the Maccabean period. But, he suggested, is it not true, as our foreparents and the prophets taught, that real circumcision is of the heart? And is not the importance of the inner circumcision the power which it gives to love God with all of one's heart and soul? And further, if this argument holds thus far, as Paul is certain it does, then cannot non-Jews represent this level of faith — even without naming it as such — and thereby be considered a part of the covenant of faith?

Paul then developed this argument to its basic conclusion: Since God has revealed the divine nature to all (1:20), to Jews first, and now to non-Jews; and since there is no longer any distinction between Jew and non-Jew in terms of justification; and since circumcision is a stumbling block to the Greeks and Romans who saw it as barbaric; therefore: whoever is circumcised in heart is really a Jew, a true member of the holy covenant, and one truly circumcised. "He is a Jew who is one inwardly, and real circumcision is a matter of the heart, spiritual, not literal" (2:29).

The rabbis had much trouble with Paul on this matter of "spiritual, not literal," just as he had had problems with it prior to his road-to-Damascus experience. The rabbis saw it as tantamount to a denial of faith in God who had called them out, led them, preserved them, and saved them. While physical circumcision did not save, they saw it as a necessary outward sign, a public commitment, a symbol of identity and unity. While circumcision of the heart was not foreign to them—indeed, it was necessary—they still feared that the denial of a literal circumcision would trivialize the covenant and serve only to mock God. It was more than a "mere symbol." It was a channel of God's grace in which the relationship of the people with God was continually re-presented.

The major Christian bodies of the world today maintain much the same position as did the rabbis in Paul's day. And these Christian leaders would be shocked to hear Paul's words addressed to them concerning their observance of the sacraments.

John Wesley understood what Paul meant. On May 22, 1750 he wrote a letter to Gilbert Royce, a Baptist minister. He was concerned to protect the belief that Christ wills the salvation of all persons, baptized or not. Thus, he wrote to Royce:

> You think the mode of baptism is "necessary to salvation;" I deny that even baptism itself is so; if it were, every Quaker must be damned, which I can in no wise believe. *I hold nothing to be* (strictly speaking) *necessary to salvation but the mind which was in Christ.*[2]

Wesley would not excuse anyone for taking lightly what Jesus had seriously commanded. Nevertheless, he maintained that the importance of baptism lay in what it points to rather than the act itself, however venerable, useful, or instructive.

And so we find ourselves driven back by Paul to his original question, this time allowing the author of Numbers to state it for us:

> God is not man, that he should lie,
> or a son of man, that he should repent.
> Has he said, and will he not do it?
> Or has he spoken, and will he not fulfill it? (23:19)

Of what value, then, is circumcision? Or what advantage has the Jew? (3:1) Much in every way, Paul contends, since God entrusted them with the divine word to be proclaimed to all the nations. And even though some were faithless, though not all, God is nevertheless still faithful. Yes, he proclaims, "let God be true though every man be false" (3:4). He recognized the special vocation that was Israel's as still intact.

"Let God be true though every person be false." The question, both stated and implied, is: Does the faithfulness of God to the divine promises rely on the faithfulness of the covenant community? Or, if the people are faithless, does that nullify the necessity for God to be faithful?

This question had serious implications for the church in the 4th and 5th centuries with the heretical Donatist movement. This was a strict and legalistic party in North Africa which held that the new bishop of Carthage, who received his ordination in 311, had received that ordination from one whose hands were stained with mortal sin. It seems as though he had surrendered copies of the scriptures for destruction during a period of persecution. This group of legalists said that the ordination was invalid, and they chose a counter-bishop, Majorinus. Donatus, after whom the party was named, succeeded Majorinus. Donatus held that ordination, baptism, or the Eucharist received from the hands of one considered a traitor to the faith through mortal sin was of no value. A church council was called in 314 in which the Donatists were condemned as heretics. The council claimed that the grace of God is effective even though the priest is personally unworthy. Thus, they could say with Paul: "Let God be faithful though every person be unfaithful."

Paul found many whom he considered faithless. Some had fallen prey to the many Greek cults. Even the chief priests and scribes had sold out their religious positions of leadership in order to obtain political favors from the Roman army of occupation. This, in fact, had been taking place at least since the Maccabean period.

One of the many sects of this time was the Essenes. They

separated themselves from even their fellow Jews, claiming that they alone were the true Israel. They repudiated the priesthood and temple worship, arguing that the priests were ungodly and therefore invalid vessels for the work of God. This sounds much like the Donatist controversy. But it illustrates that Christianity was not the only group at that time trying to define the "true Jew," "true Israel," "true circumcision," etc.

Although Paul realized that there were many unfaithful to the covenant faith, he knew that there was no reason to throw the baby out with the bath. Neither did a fresh interpretation or re-presentation of God's grace in the witness of Jesus Christ necessitate the abandonment of the Torah and the prophets. In fact, it was out of such fertile ground as this that the gospel of Christ arose (3:21). Paul was evidently quite misunderstood on this point. His critics chided him: "If our wickedness serves to show the justice of God, what shall we say...? Why not do evil that good may come?" (3:5, 8) Paul does not deal directly with this question. Such a question is irresponsible for one who stands in a personal relationship to the faithful God. Robinson puts the issue in this way:

> If you know a person loves you and will go on loving you however unworthy you are, then logically you might say, "Well, it doesn't matter now how badly I treat him or her — let's make the most of this blank cheque of love." But in fact to someone actually within a real love-relationship, knowing it not from the touch-line, but from the inside, existentially, face-to-face with the other person's devotion, then the constraint is to do precisely the opposite.[3]

Paul does not answer his hecklers. Rather he comes back to the question: "What advantage has the Jew? Are *we* Jews any better off" or "at any disadvantage?" The advantage, he says, is the glorious opportunity of serving God, of being called to represent God before the nations. But vocation is not security. And to those he considered weak in faith, he throws out the challenge that as long as they continue judging others, they will be condemned by the law — especially by the commandment against idolatry! And he makes this case by quoting from scripture. David has taught that "no man living is righteous before thee" (Ps 143:2), and, "If thou, O Lord, should mark iniquities, Lord, who could stand?" (130:3).

Thus, God shows no partiality either in glory or in shame

(2:9-11). The advantage of the Jew is that the will of God was first revealed to them through the Torah in order that the whole world would realize its accountability to God. But that does not mean that Jews are any better off — or any worse off — under such justice. The self-defense that one has followed the law is empty *without* faith, without the circumcision of the heart. "There is no distinction." Jew and Gentile, clean and unclean, are all one under God's justice and mercy. Thus: "*All* alike have sinned, and are deprived of the divine splendour, and *all* are justified by God's free grace alone, through his act of liberation in the person of Christ Jesus" (3:23-24 NEB).

8

The Continuity of Salvation

Paul developed a gospel approach apart from the law and yet consistent with its intent since "the law and the prophets bear witness to it" (3:21). Harvey writes:

> A new way of understanding how a just God can yet have dealings with universally sinful men — "has been brought to light" by the creation of a new status for men. God remains just: but a function of his justice is that he has the means of giving to men, despite their sin, the possibility of a status which is equivalent to that of the just. Once this status is accepted, God's justice no longer involves inevitable retribution for sin.[1]

This justification of God is a social phenomenon which centers in reconciliation: "There is no distinction." Paul did not see himself destroying the law, but rather restoring it to its life-giving, non-divisive character. If all must be equal under the law and before God, including "the stranger within your gates," then all are equally judged by it — to the degree it has been revealed to them.

Jesus made reference to the rain falling on the just and the unjust. In this he illustrated that God shows no partiality in sustaining creation. If we follow that to its conclusion, we must see that God equally blesses the insider and the outsider, friend and enemy. Jesus believed this so deeply that he made the real test of love and faith in God the application of love's concern for the enemy, the sinner, and, as Paul developed this, the Gentile. With this in mind, we see that Jesus' reference that we be perfect as is our Father in heaven (Mt 5:48) does not mean the state of sinlessness or the correct following of the law, ritual, and/or customs, but rather the refusal to discriminate between friend and enemy in our loving concern. The profoundly significant social implications of this have *yet* to be recognized. But is is clear that my enemy and myself, the sinner and myself, the Gentile and the Jew—all are united, not through "the principle of works...but on the principle of faith" (3:27). We are bound together in our creatureliness, in a new humanity that forbids my judging another's relationship to God, my taking control or manipulating another's life, or the taking of the life of another human being. Such is idolatry.

Because of the excessive emphasis of Paul's attack on the law, it is essential that we realize that what Paul is attacking is not Judaism or the law as such, but the faults and wrong conceptions which have crept into it. He says that "now the righteousness of God has been manifest apart from the law." He knew well that Israel's primary relationship was based on *grace* found in the covenant, not on works. That relationship was not based on Israel's righteousness since *grace was prior to any human endeavor*, prior to the law and its demands. God had chosen Israel: "I have chosen you and not cast you off" (Is 41:9). This was the basic fact of Israel's identity. All else followed from that. Whether righteous or unrighteous, believing or unbelieving, Israel stands in a covenant relationship with God. As God says through the prophet Isaiah:

> Can a woman forget her sucking child,
> that she should have no compassion on the son of her womb?
> Even these may forget,
> yet I will not forget you (49:15).

The promises of God stand forever:

> The grass withers,
> the flowers fade;
> but the word of our God will stand forever (40:8).

Without such faith in the promises of God, Israel would have no hope since she has no righteousness in and of herself. It is God's righteousness — not Israel's — that is the source of salvation.

So it is clear that Paul's criticism is of the distortion of the law and the prophets. Paul's message that justice has now been achieved apart from the law would lack all force if such justice were not precisely the same justice which the law was intended to achieve!

We must keep in mind that Paul viewed these problems in a much broader perspective than simply the isolated individual. His message also has a cosmic dimension. He anguishes over the sin and injustice that seems to reign in the heart of every person—a collective slavery that has gained control of human history because of its lack of faith in the leading of the one and true God (1:21-25). Isolated individuals may well be just and able to fulfill the will of God with a circumcised heart. Even though Paul claims here that humanity cannot keep the law, he elsewhere proudly boasts of his personal righteousness under the law and how he is without blame (Phil 3:6)!

"But now the righteousness of God has been manifested apart from the law, although the law and the prophets bear witness to it—the righteousness of God through faith in Jesus Christ for all who believe." Here we see that Jesus Christ functions as a re-presentation of the faithfulness of God. As Paul proclaims in his second letter to the Corinthians: "that is, God was in Christ, reconciling the world to himself, not counting their trespasses against them, and entrusting to us the message of reconciliation" (5:19; see also Rom 5:10). Commenting on this verse, A. Roy Eckardt writes:

> "In Christ God was reconciling the world [kosmos] to himself"
> —but note, the world, in contradistinction to Israel, which is
> not part of the world, but part of the promise, indeed, the
> first-born of God. Israel already lives with God and serves him.
> The event of Jesus is the joy that ends the dissolution of those
> who have been without hope. Jesus, that elect Jew, is the
> Second Abraham, Abraham for the gentiles, Patriarch for the
> pagans. As the poor pagan brought into the covenant of
> promise, the Christian lives out what it means to be an adopted
> child of the Father, King of the Universe.[2]

Eckardt emphasizes that this is a theological orientation, not a traditional christological orientation. "In Christ God was reconciling the world to himself "sharply conflicts with any such idolatrous avowal as 'Christ was God reconciling the world to himself'."[3]

It is suggested by Calvin Porter[4] that the phrase "faith in Jesus Christ" is poorly translated and should be read as "faith of Jesus Christ," since the Greek genative case is used here as it is in 4:4 where the same word order is translated "faith of Abraham." The translation "in" is based on a later high christological tradition.

Seen in this way, the meaning then becomes consistent with the rest of Paul's letter which is theological in emphasis. It also becomes consistent with the record of Jesus' own witness, i.e., that the purpose of his life was to point to God, not to replace God or to become somehow equal with God. Thus, 3:22 and 3:26 refer not to faith *in* Jesus to the exclusion of faith in God, but faith that in Jesus Christ God had revealed the broader implications of his Fatherhood. In Jesus Christ we see a model of the relationship between persons and God that is universally significant. If one prefers to maintain the use of "in" for traditional reasons, which most will do, it needs to be continually kept in mind that "faith *in* Jesus" *does not carry the same material significance* as "faith *in* God." To allow it to become equivalent is both idolatrous and blasphemy!

Jon Sobrino points out in his recent book, *Christology at the Crossroads*, that it was impossible for Aquinas to ascribe faith to Jesus in any manner, since Jesus as the second person of the Godhead would have faith in himself. And that for Aquinas was preposterous:

> The object of faith is divine reality that is hidden from sight....
> Now a virtue, like any other habit, takes its image from its object. Hence when divine reality is not hidden from sight, there is no point in faith. From the first moment of his conception Christ had full vision of God in his essence.... *Therefore he could not have had faith.*[5]

The position of Aquinas is still held by many Christians today, both Protestant and Catholic. For them, divinity and faith rule out one another. Yet, Sobrino reminds us, "Christology is possible only if the Father continues to be the ultimate horizon of reality, the Son continues to be the definitive example of how human beings can correspond to the Father."[6] In this manner our reflections on Jesus become theo-logical as they point us to God and to the Kingdom of God. As we can speak of Jesus having faith, and going from faith to faith, because we affirm that his "divinity" lies not in any eternal essence but in the nature of his relationship with God and the will of God. As Sobrino again writes:

> But faith in Jesus attains its maximum radicality when we accept his path as normative and traverse it. The most radical and most orthodox affirmation of *faith in Jesus* is affirming that the

faith of Jesus is the correct way to draw nearer to God and realize his Kingdom, and then acting accordingly.[7]

Having said all that, what God did in and through the historical life of Jesus is a foundation for faith, especially for gentiles, and it therefore cannot be glossed over by Christians. Salvation through the witness of Jesus Christ is a continuation of the work of God from the beginning of creation. Jesus is an episode—albeit a normative one for Christians—in the ongoing dialogue between the divine Spirit and the entire historical process in which God seeks to evoke the fruits of righteousness. Paul affirms that through Christ *"all* are now justified by *God's* free grace *alone"* (3:23-24). No longer are Jews alone justified. And more than this, we are given the power of liberation from both temporal captivity and bondage of the spirit. How? Look at these three translations and the ways they state it:

JerB	*NEB*
and *both* are justified through the free gift of his grace by being redeemed in Christ Jesus who was appointed by God to sacrifice his life so as to win reconciliation through faith.	and *all* are justified by God's free grace alone, through his act of liberation in the person of Christ Jesus. For God designed him to be the means of expiating sin by his sacrificial death, effective through faith.

RSV

they are justified by his grace as a gift, through the redemption which is in Christ Jesus, whom God put forward as an expiation by his blood, to be received by faith.

How are we to understand this today? This idea of expiation is so foreign to us because of its relationship to the sacrificial system of religion. This term is used only three times in the entire New Testament, 1 Jn 2:2 and 4:10 where the Greek term means "to appease," and here in Rom 3:25 where the Greek means "the place of appeasement." This needs to be seen in the perspective of the covenantal context. Raymond Abba helps us here:

> Hebrew sacrifice is based upon what God does for man: it pre-
> supposes the divine initiative in redemption.... The Old Testa-
> ment sacrifices are expiatory not propitiatory.... The Cultus
> was the symbolic and sacramental means of grace through
> which the covenant relationship...was maintained and re-
> stored.[8]

He goes on to explain that the significance of the sacrificial system
included: (1) making possible the realization of fellowship with
God; (2) taking sin seriously, which breaks fellowship with God;
(3) expiation of sin and effecting of atonement; (4) suggesting the
offering of one's life as the basis of his/her fellowship with God;
and (5) making possible a social and individual approach to God.[9]

This means, then, that God is the one who provides the expiation. Luke uses this conception to mean "forgive" or "to be merciful." Therefore, expiation sacrifices are acts which recognize the
merciful nature of God. It is not that they neutralize the wrath of
God, but rather overcome alienation by faith in the effectiveness of
that which the symbolic act represents. John A.T. Robinson describes expiation in these words: it is "doing away with that alienation, that distortion in the personal relationship with God, which
sin brings and which compels men to know God's love as wrath."[10]
The expiation "does something not to God but to the sin which
distorts and sours the relationship."[11] It operates, then, to neutralize the power of sin.

Expiation also refers to the avoidance of a destruction brought
on by one's guilt (Gn 32:20). However, the presentation of a gift at
the altar can also include personal goodness and faithfulness, as in
Proverbs 16:6: "By loyalty and faithfulness iniquity is atoned for."

While we might better grasp the meaning of expiation, we
might still wonder as to why blood was so important in expiation.
For the Hebrews the life-substance, or soul, was in the blood (Dt
12:23). The price of sin (i.e., the wages of sin) was death — the
shedding of this life-substance. Sin was a break in relationship between persons, the community, and God. The meaning is that life is
thereby always threatened by sin; therefore sin always needs some
means of effecting a reconciliation and forgiveness.

Expiation, then, is the removal of sin and the guilt produced
by that sin, while reconciliation is the result when relationships are
restored. Isaiah taught that on the day of death, full atonement is
made: "Surely this iniquity will not be forgiven you till you die"

(22:14). Thus, the atoning power of death was considered great by Israel. The rabbis taught this: "All the dead are cleansed from sin by death," and "If one has repented and then dies, death destroys sin."

We have seen how many of the Jews had already, by the time of Jesus and Paul abandoned the Temple sacrificial system in favor of the more spiritual interpretation proposed by the Pharisees. In just a few short years after this letter to the Romans, the Temple was destroyed. This meant that the actual blood sacrifices could no longer be made, but this did not affect the rabbis and the synagogue. The story is told of Rabbi Josua crying out when he saw the ruined city and Temple: "Woe to us, because the place is destroyed where they atoned the sins of Israel." But Rabbi Jochannan ben Zakkai said to him: "Do not grieve, my son. We have an atonement similar to it. What is it? It is almsgiving, for it is said: 'I desire mercy and not sacrifice'."[12]

For those in Dispersion, the idea of vicarious suffering was not new. For those cut off from the Temple, the ritual was performed there vicariously for all the people. Vicarious suffering also arose later around the idea that "the righteous who suffer without being guilty, or who suffer more than their guilt requires, thereby atone for the sins of the people and ward off sufferings for others."[13] Thus, the concept of the innocent suffering for the sins of others was not new with Jesus but was already a significant factor in Judaism as a means of overcoming the destructive sense of guilt and unworthiness.

Therefore, when Christian leaders began teaching about the atoning death of Jesus Christ, the rabbis may have reacted against their interpretation, but they were well aware of its usage in Judaism. Atoning death and vicarious suffering confirm the idea of community and covenant, i.e., that the suffering and/or death of some bring the grace of God's atonement to others. However, this was not the real issue the rabbis fought against in this new Christian sect:

> The doctrine of the vicarious atonement was only one aspect of the total Christology taught by the Church; and that total Christology had already infringed the boundaries of Jewish monotheism. But divorced from the notion of a God-man, there was no reason for the Synagogue to deny the idea of a vicarious atonement. There was indeed...every reason why the Synagogue should accept such a doctrine. And the figure of

Isaac, lacking all the traits which made the Christian Christ objectionable to the Synagogue, was the ideal figure around which such a doctrine could center.[14]

Thus, the basic issue was the identification of Jesus with the very nature of God. And that was, and should be today, considered idolatrous.

Expiation, then, carried for Paul the sense of setting aside sin. Jesus was "appointed by God to sacrifice his life so as to win reconciliation through faith." God did not force him to be the sin offering or expiation sacrifice, but rather God made the faith and example of Jesus a demonstration of what faithfulness could really mean. For Paul the importance of Jesus Christ was his obedience to his faith in God. As Robinson writes:

> Paul sees Christ as going on by untiring obedience simply absorbing evil...refusing to pay it back or give it out, until on the cross he exhausts its power. There is nothing more that evil can do: it is simply finished, and still it has not conquered him in the only way evil can really conquer a man, that is by making him evil.[15]

And through that witness, the boundaries separating persons were cast down. Therefore, all who in faith allow the power that was in Christ Jesus to work within them, and who become obedient unto the gospel of God discover the meaning of justification and reconciliation.

Robinson is concerned that so much doubtful theology has been based on this section of Romans (3:21-26). He writes:

> The New Testament *never* says that God punishes Christ: in fact the verb and noun for "punishment" are only used twice each in the whole of the New Testament, and never of God or Christ. Moreover, Christ stands as our representative, not as our replacement.... His work is always on behalf of us (*hyper*) not instead of us (*anti*). Of course, Christ does something we could never do for ourselves. He is there because we are not. But he died to sin, not so that we shall not have to (as our substitute) but precisely so that we can (as our representative).[16]

Christ, then, did not die "in my place," but "on my behalf."

If we have then all been justified through this *model of faith*, Jesus Christ, we are all one. "Then what becomes of our boasting?" And Paul answers emphatically: "IT IS EXCLUDED!" The entire basis of his argument is to preserve the oneness of God, the monotheism of Judaism. But Paul cautions his Jewish readers that it is idolatrous to proclaim God as only the God of Israel. And so he instructs them:

> Is he not the God of Gentiles also? Certainly, of Gentiles also, *if it be true that God is one.* And he will therefore justify both the circumcised in virtue of their faith, and the uncircumcised through their faith (3:29-30).

If God is creator of all, he is also God of all!

9

The Faith of Abraham

In Romans we see Paul arguing for a fresh vision and the moral energy that arises from faith in God alone. This justifying faith, he says, is clearly seen in Abraham. Just because some Jews may have placed a higher reliance on outward forms or rite and ritual is by no means to suggest that there was no faith in Judaism. The clarion call from both Paul and the witness of Jesus is a return to the basics of faith. Once that is done, the outward observances will naturally fall in line. Judaism, then, has the essential ingredient of salvation —faith—but some had hidden it from hair-splitting laws that separate persons from each other and from God. It is faith in God alone that is necessary for salvation. As Paul had written earlier: "Since God is *one*, he will justify the circumcised (Jews) on the ground of their faith and the uncircumcised (Gentiles) on the ground of their faith" (3:30). Thus, both Jew and Gentile are judged on the same basis: faith in God. The fact that the term circumcision refers to Jews and uncircumcision refers to Gentiles is clear from the context of the preceeding verse: "Or is God the God of Jews only? Is he not the God of Gentiles also? Yes, of Gentiles also, since God is one...."

Does this mean that the law is overthrown? "By no means!" Paul firmly asserts. On the contrary, the law is placed on *firmer* ground. Pointing to Father Abraham, Paul realized that for Jewish readers in Rome there can be no greater authority on religious matters. If one must be circumcised and follow the law in order to be justified, then Abraham, who preceded both practices, would not be justified. Such a conclusion would be unthinkable! Paul points out that Abraham was not circumcised until quite late in life, and Moses did not come on the scene until several years after that.

73

Indeed, it was on this fact of the late circumcision of Abraham that Jews had based their practice of admitting converts into Judaism.

Paul, therefore, used this widely accepted principle of Judaism to demonstrate that the gift of righteousness was given to Abraham because of his *faith in God*, and not because of any works or rites performed. Indeed, says Paul, if Abraham had earned God's favor through good works, it would not have been called a gift, i.e., "counted to." It was his faith alone that was the fundamental basis for his being justified. God's favor, shown in his coming to Abraham, preceded even that faith!

It should be noted that James takes this very same verse of scripture and makes the opposite conclusion from Paul's. Notice that Paul is *not* saying that good works are unimportant or unnecessary; only that they in themselves have no power of justifying one before God. Good works for Paul become the natural response of faith. However, James tried to correct a misunderstanding that Paul had most certainly created for the early Christian congregations. Commenting on Genesis 15:6, James writes:

> Was not Abraham our Father justified by works, when he offered his son Isaac upon the altar? You see that faith was active *along with* his works, and faith was *completed by works....* You see that a man is justified by works and *not* by faith alone! (2:21-24)

James maintained as a Christian Jew that faith alone is dead, since in order for it to be completed, faith must issue in certain actions. Without actions, there can be no proof of faith. We can clearly see that these two men place the emphasis differently — and that emphasis is important. There is no way of reconciling honestly the differences between Paul and James at this point without doing a grave disservice to both.

Paul's intellectualism undoubtedly led him into some problems of misunderstandings. This seems to be the judgment of the early Christian community, which said of him:

> "So also our beloved Paul wrote to you according to the wisdom given him, speaking of this as he does in all his letters. There are some things in them hard to understand, which the ignorant and unstable twist to their own destruction, as they do the other scriptures" (2 Pt 3:15b-16).

The German theologian Adolf Harnack wrote that in the first two centuries of the common era no one understand Paul except the heretic Marcion, and he misunderstood him!

The passage from Genesis 15:6 did not include all that Paul means by the term "faith," but since it is apparent that as a Pharisee he believed in continuing revelation which demands continual re-interpretation, that would have been no problem for him. The fine distinctions made here by Paul will probably continue to baffle the average mind. The importance of what he is saying in this fourth chapter may be stated in the following manner:

> (1) "Our forefather," he writes in effect, "did not use his special position as an occasion for boasting before God, as you do." (2) "He did not, like you, view obedience to the Law as a means of meriting special blessings from God." (3) "In his case it was not circumcision which distinguished him from the uncircumcised, but faith which distinguished him from unbelievers. For this reason he became the father of all who believe; there is no distinction among them."[1]

Abraham's faith, then, is an example for all to follow. Since there is no distinction, and all of faith are Abraham's children, then it is clear that those who do not accept this are void of faith, do not accept the witness of Abraham, and there are no longer heirs, regardless of whether one is Jew or non-Jew.

We should read Romans 4:16–25 with chapters 14 and 15 in mind. Minear points out that there are at least six distinct links here which I will quote in length. First,

> Paul took good care to dissociate Abraham from the weak in faith, using precisely the same phrase in this connection, "he did not become weak in faith" (4:19). This was a direct attack upon those who appealed to their descent from Abraham as giving them priority in God's eyes.[2]

Second,

> The Apostle explictly asserted that Abraham did not belong to Group Three, the doubters. Here again the same phrase was utilized. "No distrust made him waiver concerning the promise of God" (4:20).[3]

Third,

> The strength of Abraham's faith did not lie in his views of holy
> days and of clean foods or in his tendency to despise other
> believers. Rather it consisted in his readiness to give glory to
> God. Such glory expressed the fact that he was fully convinced
> in his own mind (4:21; 14:5).[4]

Fourth,

> The accent on Abraham as "the father of *many nations*" (4:17)
> paralleled the picture in ch. 15 of the intention of God to in-
> clude Jews and Gentiles within a single worshipping com-
> munity where Christ's welcome of all had become the measure
> of Jewish and Christian welcome of each other.[5]

Fifth, even though faith makes all believers sons and daughters of
Abraham,

> because of its common radicality, the faith of Abraham was oc-
> casioned by one event (the promise as expressed in Gen 17:5;
> Rom 4:17) whereas the faith of the Roman Christians was oc-
> casioned by another (the death and resurrection of Jesus,
> 4:24f). The apostle's argument rested upon the *comparability*
> of God's promises and God's actions in these two events and
> upon the resulting *correspondence* in the character of faith.
> This position was bound to collide with the convictions of
> Group One, whose members gave priority to God's action in
> Abraham, which appeared to them to place a premium upon
> the righteousness which comes through works and through
> circumcision (4:1-12). It was bound to collide also with the
> position of Group Two for whom the work of Christ nullified
> the promise to Abraham and justified them in despising Abra-
> ham's descendents.[6]

Sixth, Paul emphasized "a view of faith as hoping against hope in
the power of God to fulfill his promise." Groups One and Two both
made one's faith

> subject to another man's measurement and thereby denying the
> power of God's grace. Neither was fully convinced that God

was able to do what he had promised. They were living from the past rather than the future, from mundane estimates of possibilities rather than from faith's reliance on God's power to raise the dead (4:17, 25; 14:9).[7]

10

Faith "Through" Christ

Since God is just,

AND,

since God does not condemn all

(even though there are none who are just)

AND,

since we are all justified by faith in God,

THEREFORE,

we have peace with God through the meditating spirit
of Christ Jesus.

This is the witness of the opening verses of Romans 5. The term
"through" as in the phrase "through Jesus Christ" has been an issue
in the church from the very beginning. The question for us in this
chapter is this: "Is it an exclusive term meaning 'only'; that is, 'only
by the means of Jesus Christ'"?

"Through him we have obtained access..." (5:2). Paul is not
suggesting here that Christ is to be imposed as an intermediate
authority between God and human beings. As Sandmel pointed
out, "The genuine Epistles of Paul never use the word *mesites*
[mediator] of Christ, but only of Moses, Gal 3:19-20."[1] The phrase
"through Christ" is always used by Paul in reference to the exalted,
spiritual Christ. Rather than an intermediation between persons
and God, the phrase "through Christ" refers to the witness of Jesus
Christ as the foundation for the existence of Christians.

This becomes clear when we see in 4:24 Paul defining justifying
faith as belief in God who raised Jesus to the status of exalted
Christ. As Adam lives in human nature, so Christ, the initiator of a
new age of unity, lives in the believer (5:12).

The conception of mediation (other than the mediation as a part of a priest) did not occur during the teaching ministry of Jesus. It is a concept contributed by the early church as its christology developed. Mediation is therefore a part of tradition, and a concept that has posed a continual debate within Christianity. Jesus appears to have proclaimed a religion without the need of priestly mediating, affirming that we all have direct access to the Father. This is in keeping with the teachings of Pharisaism. The developing Christian congregations, with a growing need to distinguish itself from its parent body, proclaimed a religion *with* mediation. Except for John, this concept is not used in the basic New Testament writings. To say that there can be no direct access to God outside of the Christ-witness would have been both idolatrous and blasphemous. When this idea does come to the fore, it is with the understanding that in Christ there is accomplished the decisive self-offering of God to all. The emphasis is on God's self-disclosure, not on the vehicle of that disclosure, regardless of how important that vehicle may be. It is not the vessel that is important, but the substance that fills the vessel. True, the substance needs a vessel to hold it in an understandable manner, but it is not the vessel that is ultimately significant. The substance does not need one exclusive vessel. The same is true of God's witness in Christ. It is a decisive self-offering of God that is the focus, not Jesus the vessel of that self-offering.

Therefore, we have peace with God through Christ. The gift to all who have faith in God—the God who raised Jesus from the dead—is peace, hope, endurance in suffering, and joy. "God's love has been poured into our hearts through the Holy Spirit which has been given to us." This is what Isaiah had promised:

> When the Spirit is poured upon us from on high...then justice will dwell in the wilderness, and righteousness abide in the fruitful field. And the effect of righteousness will be peace, and the result of righteousness, quietness, and trust forever (32:15a, 16–17).

That the Holy Spirit, the Spirit of God, was already upon the earth in the time of Moses and the prophets is well testified to in the Old Testament. Not only was the Holy Spirit present in the midst of the Israelites and active in the leading of Moses (Is 63:11), but the Spirit of God was that creative activity of God which "moved upon the face of the waters" (Gn 1:2) at the beginning of time. On at least seventy separate occasions the Old Testament refers to persons being filled with the Holy Spirit, the Spirit of God.

In the New Testament there appears little that is distinctively new in the usage of the concept of Spirit. Continuing the emphasis of historical Judaism, the meaning of *pneuma* includes:

> berath or wind as an invisible yet sensible phenomenon; the animating principle known by the life it imparts to living creatures; an aspect of the human self, especially its inner side unavailable to sense perception and yet central to its identity as a self and to its knowing, feeling, and willing; a state of mind or disposition; an independent reality, transcending the human and benevolent or malevolent in its working; and that divine element or power which is reserved to God and distinguishes God from all that is not God.[2]

Through this term Paul conveys the idea of God's continual presence in the everyday experiences of life. Thus, Spirit does not replace the ordinary processes of human decision-making, but rather enables those ordinary processes to function at their God-intended levels. It, then, becomes that which makes right conduct, and therefore true life itself, possible. Such enabling is often communal, often individual, but never completely private. The gifts of the Spirit are given for the upbuilding of the community.

Now, with the advent of Jesus, God's Spirit has been made a reality to all people and is available to all on the basis of faith. In the action of Jesus Christ we see the creative activity of God, the revelation of divine salvation and reconciliation, and the announcing of the Spirit of fulfillment. Peace, hope, and joy are so deeply rooted in faith in God that they not only endure in the midst of persecution, but are even increased through suffering. The assurance of divine love is increased as one is forced to rely on God alone. Viktor Frankl, a Jewish psychiatrist who lived through the hell of a Nazi concentration camp, writes:

> The truth is that among those who actually went through the experiences of Auschwitz, the number whose religious life was deepened — in spite, not to say because, of this experience — by far exceeds the number of those who gave up their belief. To paraphrase what LaRochefoucauld once remarked with regard

to love, one might say that just as the small fire is extinguished
by the storm whereas the large fire is enhanced by it — likewise a
weak faith is weakened by predicaments and catastrophes
whereas a strong faith is strengthened by them.[3]

The psalmist knew well that this kind of endurance leads to hope:
"Weeping may tarry for the night, but joy comes with the morning"
(30:5b).

"While we were yet helpless, at the right time Christ died for
the ungodly.... But God shows his love for us in that while we were
yet sinners Christ died for us" (5:6, 8). Look at the development
here in 5:6–11:

> 6: We were *all* once helpless,
>> but now Christ has died for the ungodly.

> 7: One might die for a good person (or for the righteous),
>> but God shows his love for us by the death of Christ.

> 8: We are *all* now justified,
>> and saved from the wrath of God's judgment.

> 9: While we were enemies of God,
>> God reconciled us to himself by the death of Christ.

> 10: Now that we are justified,
>> we shall be much more saved by his life.

> 11: Now we rejoice in God through Christ,
>> through whom we have been reconciled to God.

The "we" referred to here is to "all of us — Jew and Gentile alike." We
were all once helpless and weak. Christ died to demonstrate God's
love for all regardless of any merit. We are all justified and freed
from the consequences of not being justified. We have been reconciled to God. Paul's emphasis here again speaks of the removal of
the barriers between the weak and the strong, both of whom tend
to deny that God's love extends to the other. All can now join together in praise to God and in devotion to the Kingdom of God's
righteousness.

We were *all* once *weak*, i.e., without faith. "Weakness" was the label used by the strong to show their contempt for Christian Jews, and unfortunately Paul was not free from the bias which this term implies. Minear writes: "I believe that in 5:6 it would have its maximum force as a reminder to Group Two concerning the universal state of all believers when Christ died for them."[4] On the other hand, Paul also used the term "sinner" in 5:8 as "the epithet used by Group One in condemning members of Group Two. This was their excuse for judging those Christians (14:3, 10, 13) and for trying to convert them to a descent respect for the law (2:12–24). Apart from such conversion, these sinners were destined for nothing but the wrath of God."[5]

Christ has broken down the barriers, the distinctions, and antagonisms made by these judgmental Christians by declaring that ALL persons are *weak and sinners*, and then by showing how God has justified ALL. Minear points to the term "boasting" in verse 11 and says:

> Paul attacked the pride which both groups took in their special standing by asserting over and over again that it was only through Christ, only through strength furnished by God's grace, and only through hope and faith (and not through their own separate status).... By dying for us when we were "sinners" or "weak," Christ had destroyed our reliance on our righteousness or our strength.[6]

By no longer relying on our own righteousness, but only on the grace of God's faithfulness, the Spirit enables us with a confidence that our present sharing in God's salvation will not be exposed to ultimate embarrassment at our death. And so we rejoice, we exalt — indeed, we boast about the faithfulness of God!

11

Newness and the Second Adam

In the second half of Romans 5 (12–21), Paul deals with the universal image of the First and Second Adams. These images would have been more clearly understood by the Gentiles, whereas the image of Abraham spoke more directly to Jews.

Adam was the type of Christ who was to come later. Typology relies on a view of history which, although not cyclical as such, does move in a loop-like repetitiveness toward the goal of history. What happened before will likely occur again when the times are right. Thus, this view of history might loop something like this:

Adam   Moses Elijah Jesus

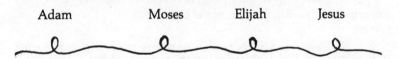

What happened in an earlier loop is a type of what will happen in the future, and when the contemporary event takes place it is considered the antitype. If one does not know all that happened in the recent contemporary loop there is no need to worry, since the details can be reasonably filled in by referring to the earlier loop, the type.

This might be illustrated in the way that the gospel writers dealt with the events surrounding the birth of Jesus. Since they did not know much about his early life, the gospel writers simply filled in the spaces by referring back to the early life of Moses, i.e., the death of male infants, going to Egypt, wilderness temptations, fasting in the desert, delivery of a new law from a mountain, etc.

Max Wilcox points to this conception of history in reference to the use of Dt 21:22–23 in the New Testament. He argues that such a

usage is to be understood as part of "an early Jewish-Christian
midrashic exposition of the *Akedah*," which was to show the connection between the roles of Isaac and Jesus. This was not an
attempt to misuse the Old Testament but was according to current
historical method. Therefore, the mixing of the images is not coin-
cidental but intentional.[1]

In typology, repetition and climax are important. In the move
from type to anti-type there is a sense of historical continuity of
past and present, as well as the basis for the future. But as Käsemann writes:

> it is not the continuity of a development which it brings out
> but, through the correspondence or antithesis of beginning and
> end, the pivot of history. Here attention is not directed towards
> the individual as example but towards whatever is pregnant
> with destiny, which spreads over into individual existence.
> Typology has a cosmic dimension....[2]

In typology one discerns certain patterns in history which enables
one to predict the future. It is on this foundation that apocalyptic
thought is based. In typology current events/persons are compared
to important events/persons of the past.

> In the past it was possible to interpret events in a cause-effect
> relationship, assuming that God brought about the effect in the
> past and would do it again whenever human beings produced
> the same cause. In partial contradiction to this was the belief
> that all events were predetermined and destined to take place at
> certain specific times, regardless of human effort. Tied together
> with the Exodus from Egypt, for instance, was the persecution
> of Hebrews by Pharoah, the establishment of a Hebrew in a top
> position of the government who was more loyal to his Hebrew
> kinspeople than to his country. Jews worked arduously to get
> their members into such positions, but they believed that God
> would raise up such people even if they failed.[3]

Thus, the situation in which the people found themselves was enhanced by the similarities between the past and the present, by an
analogy in which they saw the hand of God at work. And when the
Old Testament text was referred to for guidance, its original context was often modified to fit the present experience. But we must

not see this as dishonesty on their part. If the process of revelation is continually open, then God's new insight for today may necessitate some accommodation. And in our task of interpreting we must remember that the writers of the Christian movement read their Bibles in a different way from modern readers.

> To modern critical scholarship their way of reading the Old Testament often appears quite arbitrary in that it disregards the sense and context of the original. Yet if we are ever going to discover the sense in which such writers used their scriptures and the presuppositions which they brought to the reading of them, their quotations of the Old Testament must be analyzed along the lines...of a comparison of the text and context in which they occur with the text and context of the original.[4]

Another basic issue involved with typology is the concept of time. For biblical writers, time was seen in terms of quality, not quantity. It was for them a matter of knowing the kind of time. As Nolan writes: "when the individual reaches a fixed point...he becomes in a sense *contemporaneous* with his ancestors and his successors who have passed or will pass through the same qualitative time."[5] Thus, regardless of how many years may have intervened, one celebrates every Passover festival as though for the first time. And in the same way, the future may also be definitive, and all of our present events are measured in terms of it. For Paul, the resurrection falls in this category. While we are now resurrected with Christ, we still look toward the resurrection of the entire cosmos in the eternal life of God.

Reflecting on this, we realize that our present-day interest in scientific language and fact in dealing with history was not shared by Paul and the biblical writers. Rather they were interested in the meaning behind the story or image. The image was only the vehicle for a larger truth. Such a meaning was built into the creation stories: "adam" literally means "man" or "human." The Apocalypse of Baruch, written in the first century of the common era, says: "Each of us has been the Adam of his own soul."

Richard Rubenstein has written that for the Jewish mystics of the years just prior to and after the beginning of the common era,

> the exile condition of Israel was seen as a profound metaphor for the exilic condition of all mankind. Insofar as every life

partakes of the contrast between existence as it is and as it ought to be, Jewish exile was often interpreted as a symbol of the inherently flawed condition of human existence.[6]

In this mystical system, "the cosmos itself was interpreted as an alienated segment of God's hidden, primordial ground and in which the goal of existence was regarded as the restoration of all things to that ground."[7] He viewed Paul's discussion in 5:12–21 as "a reflection on the exilic nature of unredeemed humanity" saying that to this extent Paul was in agreement with his Jewish contemporaries.[8]

This view that was contemporary with Paul can be seen in II Esdras (3:21–22; 4:30; 7:48), as well as in Philo and other educated Jews of the time who accepted the Adam story as an allegory. The Adam story, they all taught, refers to the universality and solidarity of sin:

> We are formed to personality, brought to moral consciousness, in and through a social order which is already self-centered rather than God-centered. Therefore we are called into a personal existence which is distorted before ever we make a conscious moral judgment; We are brought up by imitation and reaction to look after number one.... [Sin] is woven into the very texture of humanity as we know it, so that we are not like Adam in the myth perfectly free to choose either *good or evil*.[9]

Therefore sin is much more than the wrong-doing of an individual. "It is an objective and corporate condition of having-gone-wrongness, of having missed the mark, got off-centre, which means that man lacks the crowning glory, the true divine humanity, which should be his."[10]

We have said that Adam was the type of Christ who was to come. Paul uses this term in 6:17 which the RSV translates as "standard." Here in 5:14 the term means a model which expresses a rule or an advance presentation. Adam, then, is an "advance presentation" which God initiated in order to point to the universal nature of the salvation which was to come in Christ. As Paul wrote in his first letter to the Corinthians: "For as in Adam all die, so also in Christ shall all be made alive" (15:22). An advance presentation points to a higher form, and as Paul indicated, a form which produces an opposite or mirror impression. The NEB translates the word as "foreshadow." In this sense, the shadow is less important than the reality to which it gives evidence.

Various types are mentioned in the prophets as well as in the New Testament writings. These include the new exodus, the new covenant, the second kingdom of David, the new Zion, the new Jerusalem, and the new creation. Such thinking was highly suitable for the centuries surrounding the era. It was not at all uncommon that the people wondered if Jesus was the second Elijah, since Elijah was to return in the age of the Messiah. In typological thinking, the age of salvation is seen as a renewal of earlier signs of salvation, only on a higher plane.

In 6:17 the reference to "type" or "standard" means "example, mould, norm, or pattern." Here it refers to Jesus as the example of faith. The model makes an impression, and in so doing it bears witness to the reality which moulded it, i.e., God. Paul refers to himself as a type or model to be followed. Thus, Paul is saying that the more one is moulded by the example of Christ, the more one will in turn become a model for others. More specifically, the reference in 6:17 is to obedience to the pattern of teaching to which one is made subject or which has been handed on. The teaching of Jesus becomes the type or norm which makes an impression so that the behavior and lifestyle of a person conforms thereto.

As we said, for Paul and many of his contemporaries, Adam is "everyman." As sin controlled the decision of Adam, so sin controls the lives of those who would live outside of faith. "Through one man sin entered the world." This is not a reference to the physical nature of one called Adam, but rather in the mythical Adam we see representative humanity. Thus, "Adam" points to a social bond, not a physical relationship. Adam's sin was disobedience to God's word. But with Moses came the Law and a multiplying of sin as the explanation of what constitutes sin is itself multiplied. Thus, both before and after Moses, persons were conditioned by sin and its power. It is interesting to note that he does not say, nor did Judaism, that sin was part of the human essence, or even natural in creation. The Calvinist doctrine of the total depravity of human nature is foreign to scripture. Rather as Paul says, sin *entered* the world, that is, sin and evil do not naturally belong to human nature or even creation.

It is through Augustine's struggle with the concept of original sin that our own concepts of sin are largely molded. Mani and Pelagius represent two points of view with which Augustine

wrestled and then drew his own ideas. Mani explained all evil as a
negative principle which is eternally opposed to the goodness of
God. Thus, there was a

> radical separation between this world, where evil naturally
> dominated, and divine reality. By fixing the origin of evil in the
> fall of souls, sparks of the divine fallen into matter, Mani simul-
> taneously indicated his idea of salvation: separation from this
> material, evil world, which is eternally opposed to the principle
> of light.[10]

Pelagius, on the other hand, saw that each of us is our own Adam,
and each new life begins a clean history of its relationship with
God. Thus, reasoned Pelagius, "if each of us is his own Adam and
inaugurates his history with God in a first innocence, if no one is
naturally guilty, what was the meaning of Christ's death for the sin
of all?"[11]

   In working out his interpretation of the origin of sin, Augustine had to avoid both conclusions. He dealt with this dilemma by
placing an excessive emphasis on the effects of that "first sin" on all
human freedom to do otherwise. The Manichaeans had "pushed
Augustine to historicize evil, in spite of his tendency to think of it
as a structure of freedom; the Pelagians led him to amplify the consequences of Adam's historical act to the point of making the
present chain of freedom into a fatality."[12] We can avoid all three
options if we realize that sin is not transmitted by a biological
process but rather by a social process. This should be relatively
easy for the twentieth century person who no longer believes in a
literal Adam and Eve. And instead of talking about original sin we
should more properly speak of the "sin of the world," for, as
Duquoc writes: "The 'sin of the world' designates the tangle of re-
sponsibilities and errors which constitute human reality in its recip-
rocal interdependences as deaf to the appeal from God."[13] Sin is
therefore not only personal but also collective.

   If, then, Adam is the symbol or type for every sinner, Christ
becomes the symbol or type of the new humanity which God has
justified *despite* its sin. Great was the sin, but greater was the grace
of God.

   Before going on, we must emphasize once more the corporate
images used by Paul in dealing with justification, sin, etc. Adam
and Jesus are not isolated individuals for Paul. While they may

have that characteristic, they both stand for the whole of humanity. Whatever historical reality there may be, it is the symbolic reality that is primary. Indeed, Paul rarely refers to the historical Jesus, and when he does it is in relation to the crucifixion which he then immediately ties to the cosmic implications of the resurrection.

"But the free gift is not like the trespass." Jesus had taught this principle by saying: "Whoever would be first among you must be your slave" (Mt 20:27), and "whoever humbles himself like this child, he is the greatest in the kingdom of heaven" (18:4). The free gift is not earned, nor even demanded, but humbly accepted.

"Then as one man's trespass led to condemnation for *all* men, so one man's act of righteousness leads to acquittal and life for *all* men" (5:18). If God loved us so much as to accomplish our acquittal even while we were weak in faith, even while we were sinners, how much more will that love be ours as the work of salvation is completed in us now that we have been reconciled to God through the divine love demonstrated in the death and resurrection of Jesus Christ.

We have been reconciled through Jesus Christ. As Gentiles who were once considered sinners and cut off from the promises of God, we have now been reconciled and brought into the covenant of Abraham. What does the term "through" mean? The Greek for "through," is translated by these other terms: "with, by means of, through the example of, through the mediation of." As indicated in an earlier chapter, the formula "through Christ" indicates that in Jesus we see the action of God's creativity in uniting all into the covenant by faith. Jesus is never seen as an intermediate authority between God and humanity whereby the authority of God is lessened and/or compromised. The formula phrase is always used in connection with the exalted Christ, the resurrected or spiritual Christ. Thus, it does not mean the end of God's direct revelation, but rather it indicates that an act of God in Christ underlies the existence and actions of the Christian, especially Gentile Christians. This is nowhere more clearly stated by Paul than in 4:24 where he defines justifying faith as *belief in God* who raised from the dead Jesus our Lord.

What about the contention that salvation comes through Jesus Christ *alone*? Again, our problem is that we place on the New Testament our twentieth century methods of thinking and are therefore led away from the meaning of Paul's message. One of the feminist contributions to theology is that "the idea of the incarnation exclusively in the male Jesus serves to inhibit an adequate understanding of the being of God. [Thus] Mary Daly accuses Christian theologians of 'Christolatry' and 'idolatry' in relation to the person of Jesus."[14] Paul's emphasis on the exalted Christ has the potential of leading us away from the exclusive maleness of the vehicles of God's revelation. For Paul, Christ is a more abstract term since it is understood as the function of God's spirit within human life. Now, if this be true, there is a distinction to be made between salvation through the Christ function of God's spirit within humans and structures, and salvation through Jesus.

The concept of "newness" is closely associated with our discussion of salvation through Christ. "New" is a theological (salvation-oriented) term of promise which refers to the goal of hope. The future is in some degree reflected in the present; and the future thereby becomes the guiding source for the present. In this manner the future hope is present and operative in the now of the present. The Hebrew root word, "HDS," is used to form such words as new, newness, new moon/moon, renew, and is obviously basic to Jewish thought and the Jewish calendar. Like the moon, Israel is renewed even though it remains the same Israel in its many transformations. Hope for the new future draws strength from the past. And this ongoing dynamic of the old and the new finds witness in the creative flux of human life and history.

Paul talks of newness in terms of the completely different force, or at least previously undisclosed in its fullness, which is now available to Gentiles. Newness is the unity of gift *and* task, of ritual *and* duty in love. And this, he says, leads naturally to the new life to be found in Christ. This speaks of a condition in the actual life of the person of faith. Faith is not just an emotional experience. It is rather an almost unconscious obedience to the Source, Guide, and Goal of all that is. This new relationship of reconciliation results in a new type of life for believers as they relate to every other person. They have been liberated from death's power and sin's control. Life is given an eternal quality that is not diminished by death.

12

Baptized into Christ

"Why should we be faithful if God is going to do all these good things for all persons?" This is a question that began to worry many Christians when they saw where Paul's teachings could lead. With his declaration of universal justification, it was only one more step to universal salvation. And so they asked: "Are we to continue in sin that grace may abound?" (6:1). "Are we to sin because we are not under the law but under grace?" (6:15). But Paul's emphatic answer is "No! If you have been freed from sin, then free indeed you are!"

"We have been baptized into Christ.... We were buried with him by baptism into death" (6:3-4). What does it mean to be baptized? Baptism has the following meanings: "to dip, to dye (clothes), to sink (in mud), to drown, to perish, to bathe, to wash." The rite of baptism is found in some form in most of the world's religions. In Judaism it was the rite administered to Gentiles converting to Judaism. The proselyte was considered a "new-born child," a term to which Paul makes frequent reference.

When we look to the gospels for help, we see that John the Baptist practiced a baptism much like that administered to Jewish proselytes. It was a once-for-all rite that made great ethical demands on its recipient. John's baptism made the idea clear that until the ethical obligation is accepted, one is considered along with the defiled Gentiles. Therefore John was already moving away from a purely ritual definition. As in Judaism, John's baptism is understood as an initiatory rite. And both incorporated the meanings of a cleansing bath. Jesus does not baptise anyone, and neither do we find that his disciples baptized during his lifetime. After all, had not John said that the baptism of Jesus would be, not

91

by water, but by the Holy Spirit? Paul claimed that he was not called to baptize, i.e., to make converts, but to proclaim a gospel of reconciliation.

We are baptized into Christ. The eighteenth century theologian, H.S. Reimarus, is helpful as we look at the meaning of this phrase. He wrote:

> the Jews considered the newly converted as newly born babies who came into an entirely new situation...[and] had to walk as Jewish members in an entirely different people and family, and had to have a new name. In that case they were simply baptized *in the name of Jewish members* (*gerim*), that is, that they would henceforth be called Jewish members and would really enjoy all of the privileges of the Jewish people.[1]

Thus, to be baptized in the name of another person, as being baptized in the name of Christ, "first of all means really to baptize someone in order for him to receive and accept a certain designation of a person or thing. In the second place, it means that he may also be and enjoy those things which the name involves."[2]

We are baptized into Christ — we are initiated into the way of Christ Jesus, into the inclusiveness of his witness. Since baptism shares the character of Christ's death (6:10), it is a once-for-all rite which symbolizes our death to the power of sin and our being exalted with Christ in his exaltation. As Gentile Christians it means that we have a new name and are made a part of the Jewish family. We share a common heritage and a common destiny. We are so "impressed" with the mark of the significance of the Christ-event that we are fashioned after it in goal and purpose.

"We shall certainly be united with him in a resurrection like his" (6:5). Again, our historically-oriented minds want to know what *actually* happened on that first Easter morning. But such a question is foreign to the gospel narratives. While they may ask the question, it is left open. The stories they tell are for specific "evangelistic" reasons. Let us briefly look at Paul's understanding of resurrection.

Paul includes himself as among those to whom the risen Christ had appeared. He says that he had seen the risen Christ in the same way as did the twelve, the 500, and James (1 Cor 15:5-8). He makes no mention of an empty tomb, most probably because these stories arise from a later tradition. We must conclude that the resurrection

for him is not empty tombs or revitalized physical bodies, but is a
spiritual event which speaks of the exaltation of Christ. As Norman
Perrin summarized for us:

> In some way they were granted a vision of Jesus which con-
> vinced them that God had vindicated Jesus out of his death,
> and that therefore the death of Jesus was by no means the end
> of the impact of Jesus upon their lives and upon the world in
> which they lived. Very much to the contrary, since Jesus as
> risen commissioned them to new tasks and to new responsi-
> bilities, they found confidence in themselves and in the future
> of the world in which they lived precisely because they were re-
> sponding to Jesus as risen, and because they were now living in
> a world in which Jesus was risen.[3]

Paul's understanding of the resurrection is obviously much closer to
that of Mark, although he pre-dates Mark by some 25 years. For
Mark, the purpose of the resurrection story is closely tied to the
story of the Transfiguration (9:2–8), whereby Mark sees Jesus as in
heaven with Moses and Elijah awaiting the time of his return as Son
of Man. Not physically revived bodies, but an *exalted* spirit is the
witness of both. Risen and Exalted are synonymous for Paul.

Because we have been buried with Christ in our baptism and
have been resurrected with him in our faith, we are now dead to the
power of sin. "For sin will have no dominion over you, since you
are not under law but under grace" (6:14). Paul's argument is not
with the law per se, but with the way that the law had been mis-
used to the point where it prevented love of neighbor and a true
sense of inclusiveness. Paul suggests that sin is not merely individual faults, but a basic rebellion against God. Any interpretation of the law which suggests a balance sheet of good deeds against
bad deeds means that one is attempting to justify oneself, a function reserved for God alone. Rightly understood, the law prevents
any success in one securing or earning righteousness before God.
Faith in God is the only way. Here Paul finds himself correcting
what he considers a misinterpretation and a misuse of the law.

You are now slaves of God (6:22). One of the distinctive
features of Greek self-awareness was the thought of freedom and
personal dignity. Slavery, on the other hand, was allowing an alien
will to take precedence over one's own. What is repudiated in
slavery is service which has no possibility of evading the task

required. The right of personal choice is absent in slavery. Paul had been educated with the influence of this Greek thought-system. But he carries it on to its logical development. Everyone, he says, is so basically controlled by death-dealing forces that they cannot do anything to overcome them. Thus, they are slaves to sin. The status of those of faith is that they are given the power to overcome this slavery to sin and its consequent separation from God. This power and freedom comes from God and is seen in the life, death, and resurrection of Jesus Christ. To be a slave of God (or of the exalted Christ) is to be in a relationship of responsibility, a relationship which God initiates and which, finally, allows for the option of true choice.

13

Sin Excludes — Spirit Includes

In the seventh chapter of his letter, Paul turns to address the Christian Jews who are familiar with the law. For his Gentile readers he had established that being baptized into Christ means that one has died to sin. Now for his Jewish readers he states that baptism into Christ involves a death to law. Both Jew and Gentile are to enjoy a freedom from former bondage. The example Paul uses to drive home this point is the marriage relationship.

The law is binding only during one's lifetime. Thus, at the death of her husband, a wife is free from the law which bound her to him. In the same way a person's duty to the law ceases at death. In both cases, death brings about the possibility of a new relationship. When we are incorporated into the body of Christ — that is, the community which is elsewhere described as the bride chosen by God for the bridegroom, Christ — we are free to "bear fruit for God." The sexual imagery cannot be dismissed here. The marriage will result in good issue — good works. As in the best of Judaism, these good works are never the *ground* of our acceptance by God but the response to that acceptance.

"While we lived on the level of our lower nature, the sinful passions evoked by the law worked in our bodies, to bear fruit for death" (7:5). And what did such loyalty to the law suggest to Paul? It led them to think more highly of themselves than they ought. It had caused them to think that because they followed the law more closely than others that they were therefore more favored by God. Thus, in the past it made them condemn others; now it carried over as a disruptive force in the congregations. If they continued to set themselves up as judges over others because of their justification through the law, they would remain in bondage and "bear fruit for

death." However, it need not be that way. "Having died to that
which held us bound, we are discharged from the law, to serve God
in a new way, the way of the spirit, in contrast to the old way, the
way of a written code" (7:6).

To these Christian Jews, Paul's words must have sounded
strange. At its best Judaism had not seen the fulfilling of the law as
a burden, much less a means of bearing the fruits of death! The law
was a gift from a gracious God, and it was a joy to serve the Al-
mighty through it. However, as Sandmel points out, the Greek influence on Judaism did cause some problems for those living in
Dispersion, as did Paul. "The Law of Moses was a problem to
Hellenistic Jews from both an internal or practical consideration
and also from an external or theoretical one. Internally, the state of
affairs presupposed and explicitly set forth in the Law was this: the
Temple in Jerusalem was central and focal."[1] But what of those who
lived in distant places and could not make the long and expensive
pilgrimage to the Holy City. Undoubtedly, Paul "faced the contradiction that he studied and read in the synagogue scriptural legislation which he and other Jews were not fulfilling, for the simple
reason that for them the legislation had fallen into disuse."[2] The
Judaism of Paul, then, was no more like biblical Judaism than
present-day Christianity is like the first generation congregations.
Therefore, Paul falls back on his argument that the written law
demands of Christian Jews things that they could not fulfill.

Now he does not make any identification between law and sin.
He affirms that the law is holy and a gift from God. But, he insists,
if it were not for the law, a person would never know the meaning
of sin, especially the sin which has made them exclusive as opposed
to inclusive.

Then Paul introduces the illustration of the sin of coveting.
Minear argues that there is good reason for choosing this example:

> He had used the same Greek work in 1:24 to refer to the basic
> sin of the Gentile world — their refusal to honor God as God
> and to give him glory, gratitude, and wisdom. He had also used
> it in 6:12 referring to Gentile Christians who were tempted to
> use the new life in the Spirit as an alibi for uninhibited behavi-
> our. In 13:9 the prohibition of covetousness was used in im-
> mediate conjunction with the command to love the neighbour,
> an action which accomplished the fulfillment of the whole Law.
> This suggests that coveting was a form of hating the neighbour.[3]

If this specifiic example is elsewhere used in reference to Gentile Christians, why does Paul use it here as an example to Christian Jews? Because he saw in their judgmental attitude a presumption "upon the kindness of God" (2:4). Thus, "the commandment which *should have* led to life proved *in my experience* to lead to death" (7:10). The law, which is "holy and just and good" was used by sin to bring about an evil purpose.

These Christian Jews were condemning their fellow Christians, especially the Gentiles, by claiming superiority on obedience to the Law. And Paul responds to this by denouncing any claim to special favor before God and the right of judging others. The law does not cause death, but shows the degree to which sin reigns in one's life. It reveals that "I am unspiritual" and "the slave of sin." Within each person there is the ongoing battle between the law of God, the law of sin, and the law of reason. Unless the Spirit of God as seen in Christ frees us from such inner conflict, one is led to despair.

Likewise, law permeates our social structures and is the hallmark of civilization. Its power holds sway over all people and even increases its grasp. We are slaves to sin, even though we believe that by observing the law we are struggling against evil. Law alone makes us believe that through our own unaided efforts justice will be established upon the earth. Our striving for justice is not evil or sinful — indeed, it is essential — but sin uses that striving to fulfill the law to produce in us "all kinds of wrong desires" (7:8) based on self-interest. The law is finally forced by us to promise what it cannot deliver: it can condemn, but it cannot destroy sin.

This argument is not unknown to us. It was used by the advocates of racist policies during the Civil Rights Movement since the mid-50s. It was argued that one cannot legislate love, i.e., that through law one cannot force another to be loving. When left at this point, it becomes obvious that the law was being forced to include something that it does not profess. The intent of the law is to make equality of rights the base expectation. Hopefully, law would provide an atmosphere where love of neighbor would be possible. But the creation of such love was not its intent.

So it was with Paul. He is arguing that the people have demanded from the Law something which it is not designed to give. The purpose of the law was not to win God's grace — that is a free gift of God. Rather, the purpose of the law was to provide a means of human response to that grace and to provide the context in which that grace might take on a wider area of influence.

Therefore, if one does not recognize the function of the law, its form can be used by sin for evil purposes. "The law is spiritual," says Paul, "But I am not. I am unspiritual, the purchased slave of sin. I do not even acknowledge my own actions as mine." It is not my fault, we may be led to say. I was only following orders – the response made to atrocities in every war. "What I do is not what I want to do, but what I detest." My actions do not reflect my true desires, but are done against my true will. I couldn't help myself. After all, I'm only human. "But if what I do is against my will, it means that I agree with the law and hold it to be admirable." If in obedience to the law I do things which are against my will, I am admitting that the law is right and I am wrong. Or if the law demands that I do certain things which are not in my power, such as the Temple sacrifices while I am living in a distant land, then I again hold that the law is right and I am wrong. "But as things are, it is no longer I who perform the action, but sin that lodges in me." If in obedience to the law I do things which I do not agree with, then it is sin which controls my actions. "For I know that nothing good lodges in me – in my unspiritual nature, I mean – for though the will to good is there, the deed is not. This good I want to do, I fail to do." I want to fulfil the law and do what it instructs, but I find it impossible. And, "what I do is the wrong which is against my will; and if what I do is against my will, clearly it is no longer I who am the agent, but sin that has its lodging in me." The commedian Flip Wilson made the phrase popular which well describes this part of the complaint: "The devil made me do it." It is not something that I do, but something that controls me.

Thus, the struggle is between "the law that my reason approves" and the "law of sin." However, the last word in this battle is with God alone, and God rescues "me out of this body doomed to death...through Jesus Christ our Lord!"

The law excludes. The spirit includes all. It is not that they are opposites, but that they perform separate functions, both of which are necessary. Sin uses the position of chosenness, which is good and holy in itself, to exclude others, which is evil. The law which was revealed to a chosen group by God in order that they might become the light of his faithfulness to all the nations. But sin uses that chosenness to form those persons into an exclusive group who hold that they alone possess salvation. Through the law sin makes us covetous, we refuse to honor God's will, and we refuse to be channels of God's divine glory to the world in which we live. The law is used for privilege, status, uninhibited individualism, refusing to love our neighbor, and claiming that because we have done all that the law requires and are successful, everyone else can do the same.

Coveting uses the law for the sinful purpose of self-aggrandizement. However, the true purpose of the law is to build up the community and to give each individual a sense of responsibility for the entire community. The Rabbis had taught that in wronging another human being, one has committed an offense against the majesty of God. They had also taught that "the letter kills, but the spirit gives life." Undoubtedly, Paul was relying on this lesson that he had learned in the synagogue at Tarsus. Indeed, the rabbinic traditions included the teaching that "God himself is each day expanding the scope and insight of Torah."[4]

The significance of Paul's use of the conception of coveting can be seen in comparing Romans 7:7–24 and Genesis 3:1–24. The first law was given in the second creation story and was directed against the sin of coveting: "You shall not eat of the fruit of the tree in the midst of the garden, neither shall you touch it, lest you die." Sin, in the image of the serpent, tried to find a way to use the law for an evil end. Playing on Adam's and Eve's desires, the serpent finds a way by arguing for the love of God over against his wrath. Without the law, says Paul, there is no sin. If we replace the term "sin" with "serpent" we see that Paul's argument is not so new after all. It also provides an answer to the issue surrounding the introspection and guilt-ridden interpretations of Romans 7:15–24.

Romans	*Genesis*
7:7b: If it had not been for the law, I should not have known sin. I should not have known what it is to covet if the law had not said, "You shall not covet."	2:16–17: You may eat from every tree in the garden, but not from the tree of knowledge of good and evil; for on the day that you eat from it, you will certainly die.
7:8: But sin, finding opportunity in the commandment, wrought in me all kinds of covetousness. Apart from the law sin lies dead.	3:1: The serpent was more crafty than any wild creature that the LORD God had made. He said to the woman, "Is it true that God has forbidden you to eat from any tree in the garden?"

Romans	*Genesis*
	3:4–5: The serpent said, "Of course you will not die. God knows that as soon as you eat it, your eyes will be opened and you will be like gods knowing both good and evil."
7:9–10: I was once alive apart from the law, but when the command-ment came, sin revived, and I died; the very commandment which promised life proved to be death to me.	3:6b–7: She also gave her husband some and he ate it. Then the eyes of both of them were opened and they discovered that they were naked....
7:11–24: For sin, finding opportun-ity in the commandment, deceived me and by it killed me....	3:13: "The serpent tricked me, and I ate."

Just as Adam and Eve are symbols for all of humanity, so Paul's "I" reflects common humanity. Because Adam and Eve did not control their desires and ate of the trees, death was their future: "Dust you are, and to dust you shall return" (Gn 3:19). Who will deliver us from this universal death? "God alone, through Jesus Christ our Lord! Thanks be to God! (7:25a). Because of God's revelation in the exalted Christ, we learn that eternal life with God, beginning now and extending beyond our physical death, is available for all persons of faith. If our life is lived by faith in God's own faithful-ness toward us and toward all creation, we are set free from the bondage of fear and death.

14

Atonement and Freedom in Christ

Continuing to address those whom he has labelled as weak in faith, that is, those who tend to condemn others who do not follow the law as they do, Paul says that if salvation is for any, it must be for all. This follows from what he now knows of the nature of God as revealed in Jesus Christ. Indeed, "any claim to the special favour of God, any condemnation of outsiders, would illustrate that very presumption which marked the unbroken power of sin and death."[1] There is no substantial distinction between Jews, Christian Jews, and Gentile Christians, since the witness of God in Christ Jesus removes all barriers which once separated them. All bonds which once held them in captivity have been broken. As we all alike share in the universal legacy of Adam, so now we all alike share in the freedom of Christ Jesus. "The conclusion of the matter is this: there is no condemnation for those who are united with Christ Jesus, because in Christ Jesus the life-giving law of the Spirit has set you free from the law of sin and death" (8:1-2).

What the law could not do because of the exclusiveness arising from our lower natures, God has done through the inclusiveness of the witness of Christ. In Christ there is no basis for such condemnation of others in the community. Because of Christ, the law has found its fulfillment in us, that is, in those whose lives are directed by the Spirit of God. As Minear comments:

> This accomplishment had required not the condemning of men but the condemnation of "sin in the flesh." The whole argument becomes very concrete and relevant when we define this particular "sin in the flesh" as the tendency to condemn fellow-Christians as an act of the supposed loyalty to God's law.

101

Those who "want to please God" (8:8) can never please him by such an act."[2]

Unlike those followers of the law who condemn others, God revealed the divine will in Jesus Christ who was "in a form like that of our own sinfulness." Rather than being aloof from us because of his chosenness, God demonstrated divine care for us by means of our own human nature. What is it that God has done to free us from the law of sin and death? Look at 8:3 in the various translations:

NEB

...by sending his own Son in a form like that of our own sinful nature, and as a sacrifice for sin,* he has passed judgment against sin within that very nature, so that the commandment of the law may find fulfilment in us....

*Or, and to deal with sin.

RSV

...sending his own Son in the likeness of sinful flesh and for sin,* he condemned sin in the flesh, in order that the just requirement of the law might be fulfilled in us.

*Or, and as a sin offering.

TEV

He condemned sin in human nature by sending his own Son, who came with a nature like man's sinful nature to do away with sin. God did this so that the righteous demands of the Law might be fully satisfied in us....

Phillips

But God has met this by sending his own Son Jesus Christ to live in that human nature which causes the trouble. And, *while Christ was actually taking upon himself the sins of men, God condemned that sinful nature*. So that we are able to meet the Law's requirements....

JerB

God dealt with sin by sending his own Son in a body as physical as any sinful body, and in that body God condemned sin. He did that in order that the Law's just demands might be satisfied in us....

Living Bible (Para)

We aren't saved from sin's grasp by knowing the commandments of God, *because we can't and don't keep them,* but God put into effect a different plan to save us. He sent his own Son in a human body like ours — *except* that ours are sinful — and destroyed sin's control over us by giving *himself* as a sacrifice for our sins. *So now we can obey God's laws....*

It should be readily apparent that the *Living Bible* paraphrase grossly distorts the intention of this text in at least three fundamental ways. First, Taylor has failed to sense the context of this verse. Paul does not make an issue of one's inability to follow the Law, especially his own such inability. He writes in Philippians 3:6 that "as to righteousness under the law [I was] blameless" or faultless. As Stendahl points out:

> Nowhere in Paul's writings is there any indication that he had any difficulties in fulfilling what he as a Jew understood to be the requirements of the law. We often quote and preach wonderful sermons about the words of Paul, "...forgetting what lies behind and straining forward to what lies ahead, I press on..." (Phil 3:13ff). But few are those who can read their Bibles with sufficient simplicity as to understand what it is that Paul forgets: his achievements, not his shortcomings.[3]

In fact, Paul claims to have gone "from glory unto glory" (2 Cor 3:18).

Second, Paul's argument is not that Christ has freed us in order that "now we can obey God's laws." This relates to the first criticism and yet goes beyond it. That which Taylor fails to perceive is that from which Christ has set us free is the tendency to define religious experience in exclusivistic terms, that is, the tendency of our lower nature to covet the judgmental powers of God and to claim that our own experience is the standard by which all others are to be judged. Paul's argument is not against the law as such, nor is it against our inability to perform the law. His argument is that holy as the law is, it does not alone bring salvation. Salvation is a gift of God's grace through faith. The fulfillment of the law is the response of the faithful.

Third, Taylor has committed the worst kind of error — a direct mistranslation. The argument that this is *only* a paraphrase and therefore some latitude is to be granted is no argument at all, since so many accept his paraphrase as scripture. Taylor declares that the nature assumed by Christ was not fully human: "*except* that *ours* are sinful," i.e., the human nature of Christ is not like ours because he was perfect and sinless in every way. Such a distinction completely obliterates Paul's point. Paul seeks to demonstrate that sin was defeated "within that very nature." As our model of faith, it is essential that the defeat of sin be possible for us in the same way that it was defeated by Christ, that is, through faith in the faithfulness of God.

In looking at this basic criticism of Taylor, we need to consider the phrase, "sacrifice for sin." Jesus as a son of God was accepted as an agent of God's grace who could speak with the authority given him by the Father. The Son is not God—which Taylor's orthodoxy implies—but is the chosen one who would, with the help of God's Spirit, overthrow the enemies of God, specifically sin and death. While the function of Christ proceeds from God, the form is physical, human, and sinful in the sense that all humanity is the inheritor of Adam's legacy. The subject is God's action in the Son. The Son is not the subject.

All the translations agree with the terminology of Christ as a sacrifice for sin. Within Judaism suffering was an indication of forgiveness and a means of atoning that was more effective in providing a release from sin than was animal sacrifice. As Buchanan suggests, "the voluntary suffering of the Messiah was the most effective of all."[4] Buchanan also explains how the sin offering made the priest sinless:

> When the high priest functioned on the Day of Atonement, very careful efforts were made to keep him from being defiled in any way, so that he could be free from defilement. He also offered a bull for a sin offering for himself and his family so that he could be absolved from every other type of sin against God before he ministered in behalf of the people. This meant that he was legally free from sin on the Day of Atonement.[5]

As far as the popular religion of Paul's day was concerned:

> Philo claimed even more for him. He said that, in his judgment...the high priest was the child of incorruptible parents and free from any kind of defilement, since God was his father. Philo said further that when the high priest entered the holy of holies, he became more than a man, but not yet God, retaining both mortality and immortality, created and uncreated essence.[6]

While Paul does not get into the issues of the virgin birth or the human perfection of Jesus—he is not really interested in the historical Jesus—Taylor infers these into his paraphrase. However, in the sin offering made by the priest, he is made perfect in order to offer up a perfect sacrifice for the people. When that sacrifice becomes the voluntary offering of the Messiah, the atonement was the most effective of all. If for popular Judaism a more effective sacrifice could not be made, then Paul's opening verses in this eighth chapter to the Christian Jews became most meaningful. The self-sacrifice of the Messiah was effective for the sins of not only Jews and Gentiles, but for the entire created world.

This illustrates for us that Jesus was fully human and therefore sinful in the objective sense of Romans 5:12-14. There are those who will strongly object to this understanding of a fully human and therefore sinful Jesus. But we must maintain that this in no way detracts from the liturgical or ritual conception of the sinlessness of his self-sacrifice. In the death of Jesus, God passed judgment on sin — not on the sinner.

Now, not all sin is removed by this offering. The rabbis taught:

> If a man said, "I will sin and repent, and sin again and repent," he will be given no chance to repent. [If he said] "I will sin and the Day of Atonement will effect atonement," then the Day of Atonement effects no atonement. For transgressions between man and God, the Day of Atonement effects atonement, but for the transgressions that are between man and his fellow, the Day of Atonement effects atonement only if he has appeased his fellow (Yoma 8:8-9).

Jesus validated this interpretation for Christians when he taught his disciples: "So if you are offering your gift at the altar, and there remember that your brother has something against you, leave your gift there before the altar and go; first be reconciled to your brother, and then come and offer your gift" (Mt 5:23-24). Therefore, on the Day of Atonement, sin was forgiven under the following conditions: "(a) that he repent of his sins; (b) that he be reconciled with his fellow Israelite against whom he had sinned; and (c) that he bring the proper sin and guilt offerings to the altar on the Day of Atonement to pay for his sins against God.[7]

For Paul, the self-offering of Jesus Christ satisfied the fulfillment of the law of sacrifice, and he satisfied this for all persons, Jew and Gentile alike. However, all persons still had the obligation of repentance and reconciliation to those they had offended.

15

Is Christ the New Torah?

In 8:9 Paul turns his attention to those who doubt, those who waiver in uncertainty about "how much they should observe the Torah, secretly enamoured of the freedoms enjoyed by the 'strong,' fearful of being ostracized by the weak and of being cursed by God, yet responsive to the apostolic announcements of emancipation."[1] To these who want the best of both worlds but are afraid to grasp either, Paul gives the assurance that "*all* who are moved by the Spirit of God are sons of God," whether Jew or Gentile. The Spirit is of God and therefore moves with certainty. We have no need to fear our doubt our justification and salvation.

The Spirit is the Spirit of God. The "Spirit of Christ" (8:9) refers to the Spirit which was in Jesus. As we have already mentioned, Paul shows little interest in the historical Jesus. He therefore uses the term "Christ" in a more technical sense which transcends the historical life of Jesus and refers to that function of God's Spirit which was operative in the life of Jesus. For Paul, "Christ" refers to that divine activity of God, and rarely to the historical personage of Jesus. It is evident that the human career of Jesus was not as crucial for faith as was the Christ-function which was revealed through his witness. Jesus was born, he lived, and he died. The Christ, on the other hand, had always existed and always would until the time when all things are incorporated into the eternity of God's life. The critical point for the history of humanity is the unique intersection of these two. Nevertheless, it is God and not Jesus Christ who is the primary focus for Paul. Jesus Christ is not God. As Sandmel rightly argues: "It may appear to us that in Paul's view Christ acts *for* God; but in Paul's thought God acts *in* Christ."[2] Thus, Jesus Christ is not an "autonomous dispenser of salvation."

106

"Jesus Saves!" is not a slogan with which Paul would feel comfortable. "It is not Paul's belief that Christ has saved him, but rather that God has saved him through Christ."[3] In another place Sandmel suggests that Paul's understanding of the Christ was similar to the popular Hellenistic concept of "Logos" as used by Philo. If so, this was Paul's manner of speaking of "the immanent aspect of the transcendent God."[4]

This raises the question: Is Christ for Paul the new Torah? In order to arrive at some conclusion about this question, we need to remember that the Hebrew understanding of Torah was not "law" but "divine revelation" or "divine teaching." When the Bible was translated from Hebrew into Greek — the first five books around 250 B.C.E. and the rest by 150 B.C.E. — the Greek Jews gave to the first five books the title *Nomos* which means "law." That is considerably different from "divine teachings." This translation was necessary since "many more Jews lived in the Greek world than in Judea; indeed, there were more in the city of Alexandria, Egypt... than in the Holy Land."[5] Torah can mean many things:

> It can mean the Ten Commandments; it can mean the Five Books of Moses; it can mean the totality of Scripture; it can mean, in a general way, the gracious act of revelation at Sinai, as if beyond both the Ten Commandments and the Five Books. ...Torah, so we might say, takes on the force of the very fullest inheritance of God's gracious revelation. The inheritance and the possession of Torah, then, marked the difference between the Israel of God and the nations of the world.[6]

When the terminology of the legal sections of the Old Testament is examined in the context of the covenant, as an act of God's grace, and as "provisions nourishing the life of God's people," we are led to see that "legalism is foreign to the Old Testament."[7] As African theologian D.H. Odendaal writes: "Certainly in Leviticus and Deuteronomy *law is preaching*, and it continues to be such in other parts of the Old Testament.... When properly so viewed it is apparent that in the Old Testament too we have the beginning of gospel."[8]

Torah, as the fullest revelation of God's grace, was the expression of divine love and care which called for a response from every person. Torah was understood as "the continuing presence of God among his people; the Torah, indeed, was the *living* God."[9] It was the function of God in this world, and the bridge between God and humanity. Evil had no power over Torah. Torah overcame death and the power of sin, and was the power of life for those immersed in it. Thus, "in no sense was the yoke [of Torah] conceived of as an intolerable burden; rather, the figure of speech had to do with the fulness in which obedience was to be expected."[10] And E.P. Sanders emphasized that "*obedience maintains one's position in the covenant, but it does not earn God's grace as such.* It simply keeps an individual in the group which is the recipient of God's grace."[11] Thus, the yoke of the Torah was a sign of real freedom, just as for Paul being a slave for God or a slave to Christ was a sign of true freedom.

Torah is God's gift, and is to be fulfilled in terms of gratitude without any hope of getting a reward for doing so. Paul reminded the Corinthians about their gifts for the poor Christian Jews in Jerusalem: "Each one must do as he has made up his mind, not reluctantly or under compulsion, for God loves a cheerful giver" (2 Cor 9:7). Then he goes on to help them see how important for their own spiritual growth that this gift is: "Under the test of this service, you will glorify God because of your obedience in acknowledging the gospel of Christ, and by the generosity of your contribution for them and for all others" (9:13). Even though rewards and punishments are a part of our Judeo-Christian heritage, they are rarely seen as motives for right action. An essential element in our understanding of Torah, then, is the "joy of the law" which the rabbis believed could not be conceived by those who had not experienced its life-giving grace. Through observance of the law, through obedience of faith, one could give glory to God. Torah, then, is a complete gift which is given without reservation. "Nothing of the Torah, God assures Israel, was kept back in heaven. All that follows is only a matter of interpretation."[12] Paradoxically, the rabbis taught that "God Himself is each day expanding the scope and insight of Torah,"[13] since like the universe itself, Torah was created "to be a process."

The ultimate aim of Torah is that its influence will reach all persons so that eventually all Gentiles will be dedicated to the worship of the one true God. For the Torah "is not the Torah of the Priests, nor the Torah of the Levites, nor the Torah of the Israelites, but the Torah of Man (Torah ha Adam), whose gates are open to receive the righteous nation which keeps the truth and those who are good and upright in their hearts."[14] Likewise, the legends surrounding the Sinai experience point to the universal quality and purpose of the revelation. The rabbis taught that God gave the Torah "in open places, in the free desert, so that every man feeling the desire might receive it."[15]

How, then, are we to understand the apparent disparity between law and gospel in Romans? As we have seen, Torah is both gospel *and* law, both story *and* ethic, both haggadah *and* halachah. As Sanders writes:

> Early Christians, like Paul, could correspondingly devalue Torah as law since *halakot* which had been developed for obedience in an on-going life style might not all be pertinent in the intense atmosphere of anticipation of the End. But Torah as story was important to the early churches as they moved out into the Mediterrean world because of its adaptability to the Gentile mentality of Hellenistic culture.[16]

The similarities between Paul's talk about the activity of God in Christ and the rabbinical talk about the activity of God in Torah cannot be dismissed. Both are: (1) a divine revelation of God's love and grace; (2) a sign of God's continuing presence in the world; (3) a bridge (or means of continuing communication) between God and humanity; (4) a response is expected in terms of faithful obedience in a different lifestyle; (5) free from the powers of evil; (6) a power of life and salvation in the hearts of the faithful, overcoming for them the powers of sin and death; (7) a sign of true freedom; (8) pre-existence in that they emminate from the very life of God; and, (9) based on the universal purpose of bringing the world to faith in God alone.

The idea of an "embodied law" is not unique with Jesus Christ. Sandmel tells us that an embodied law was an outstanding individual who "promulgated written, specific laws for others, but he himself lived by the unwritten law of nature. Abraham, Isaac, and Jacob, Philo tells us, were laws embodied in men."[17]

While the argument for Christ as the new Torah could be made, it is more consistent with Paul's writing to speak of the divine revelatory activity that was at work in both Torah and Christ. In this way we can maintain our emphasis in God instead of the vehicle used by God. We can then see that there are here two basic *stages* of God's activity in Judeo-Christian history, although there were certainly other acts of self-revelation.

If we are to embody this life-giving revelation of God, then we must live out its meaning in our lives and in our communities of faith. Paul writes: "Anyone who does not have the Spirit of Christ does not belong to him." What is the Spirit of Christ, other than the Spirit of God that we see in the witness of Christ Jesus? It is the attitude and intention of inclusiveness in which all are justified by God, regardless of whether they are Jew or Gentile. It further means that we are all sons and daughters of God through our brother Christ. The Spirit of God dwells with us and we are given new life through it. Therefore we hear Paul say: "Moreover, if *the Spirit of him who raised Jesus* from the dead dwells within you (i.e., the Spirit of God), then God who has raised Christ Jesus from the dead will also give new life to your mortal bodies through his indwelling Spirit" (8:11).

In his characteristic manner, Taylor misinterprets the sense of 8:11 with his paraphrase: "And if the Spirit of God, who raised Jesus from the dead, lives in you, *he will make your dying bodies live again after you die*, by means of this same Holy Spirit living within you." The context of this verse is not that of physical resurrection after death, but rather new life in this present situation.

What specifically, then, does Paul mean by the terms "life" and "new life"? Briefly put, true life is knowing and doing the will of God. Like many of his contemporaries, including Rabbi Yohanan ben Zakkai, Paul was obviously influenced by the prophet Jeremiah. In the midst of struggle between many diverse groups in Judaism, Rabbi Yohanan sought help from the writings of Jeremiah, and with the later destruction of the Temple, Yohanan was able to make a significant contribution to the future direction of Judaism.

Jeremiah (31:31–34) suggested that when the law is written on tablets of stone, sin may use that law for its own purposes and thereby bring about disobedience or insincere obedience. Therefore, the "more perfect" law would be one written upon the hearts of human beings in which it would be an integral part of their total person and would thereby bring together intention and action. Because of this internal unity, there will be no need to remind each other of the need to be faithful (which is a function of law). It will be a natural relationship as the will of God and the will of the people of God become one (or at least move intentionally in that direction).

Paul clearly alludes to Jeremiah when he writes: "our sufficiency is from God, who has qualified us to be ministers of a new covenant, not in a written code but in the Spirit; for the written code kills, but the Spirit gives life" (2 Cor 3:6). References in Romans that we have already pointed out are 2:29 and 7:6. Paul bases his understanding of "life" on Jeremiah and Habakkuk: true life is the life of righteousness lived by faith in which the will of God reigns supreme. Life becomes life only in covenant relationship. Outside of the covenant context life is absent and there is only death. The common life is futile since it does not lead to anything good or lasting. The common life of the flesh "is man's life as adjusted to the demands which the earthly conditions make upon him. True life, on the other hand...is one in which the individual believer has become a member of the body of the risen Lord...."[18] Life means power to resist evil. When one comes into this relationship, whether through Torah or Christ, then even the mortal body takes on this power for good. The ultimate result is resurrection with a resurrection like that of Christ's.

"For all who are moved by the Spirit of God are sons and daughters of God." The Spirit enables us to understand that God is not someone to be feared, but someone to be trusted. The Fatherhood of God is not new with Christianity. As we demonstrated earlier, God as Father was one of the three basic teachings of the Pharisees. The term "father" in reference to God was used frequently in Jewish liturgy and rabbinic writings. (Indeed, the terminology with reference to the Motherhood of God is likewise present.) The point of Paul here is that the Spirit of God makes us children of God. Jews were already considered the sons of Abraham and the sons of God. Since Abraham's descendants are sons and daughters of God, they are free and heirs of the promises of God. Now that Gentiles are included in that inheritance, Paul proclaims that "we are God's heirs, and Christ's fellow-heirs, if we share his sufferings now in order to share his splendour hereafter" (8:17).

16

And So We Wait

In order to share in God's glory after our physical death — a joy which Christ now shares — we must share in Christ's sufferings on behalf of the world now. Elsewhere Paul speaks of the congregation as a "fellowship of suffering" (Phil 3:10). A suffering like that of Christ's would be a divine necessity willingly accepted in obedience to God's love for all of creation.

> The believers who thus accept suffering not only serve Christ's cause...but also, being united with the risen Lord, continue his suffering for mankind, because the church is his body.... In completing "what is lacking in Christ's afflictions" (Col 1:24), the believers participate...in the atoning work of Christ. Thus, suffering is the inescapable lot of the Christians....[1]

Suffering for the Christian is unavoidable since its aim is in opposition to the evil powers of this world. As we have seen in earlier chapters, the suffering of the righteous held, for Judaism, an atoning effect, and here in his Jewishness, Paul argues for the same principle. Suffering still remains a consequence of the evil in the world, but the power of God works through it to bring about a greater good (8:28). Suffering tries our faith and seeks to destroy our desire for the will of God. But the Spirit helps us conquer it and the death it seeks to produce. We are assured of our ultimate victory because of God's faithfulness demonstrated in the resurrection of Jesus Christ. This hope gives us confidence that although we may lose all that this world has to offer, what we now endure has "no comparison with the splendour, as yet unrevealed, which is in store for us" (8:18).

112

Our suffering leads us to realize that not only do we long for the day of God's total reign, but *the entire creation* yearns for fulfillment. Yes, even the created universe awaits the Day of the Lord:

> It was made the victim of frustration, not by its own choice, but because of him who made it so; yet always there was hope, because the universe itself is to be freed from the shackles of mortality and enter upon the liberty and splendour of the children of God (8:20–21).

That the universe is subjected to such frustration stems from the creation stories. Noah, who provided a remnant of humanity and animal life after the flood, was given his name by Lamech because, he said, "This boy will bring us relief from our work, and from the hard labour that has come upon us because of the Lord's curse upon the ground" (Gen 5:29).

This kinship of the whole of creation in both its glory and its frustration is matched by the "Song of the Three. This was an addition in the Septuagint version of Daniel between 3:23 and 3:24. In this majestic hymn of praise, the entire universe joins in the adoration of God.

Suffering, then, is the struggle between the evil nature of this present age and the new age to come in which the full power of God's promised inheritance is to be revealed. However, we do not have to wait completely. "In everything, as we know, he [the Spirit of God] cooperates for good with those who love God and are called according to his purpose" (8:28). Paul compared this to the cries of a woman in the onset of labor. Birth comes with pain. Isaiah referred to the birth pangs of national birth and rebirth. He considered Abraham the earthly father and Sarah the earthly mother who bore Israel (Is 51:2), while later Israel is referred to as the bride of God (54:1–6). Again, Zion which is both the "fortified hill of pre-Israelite Jerusalem" and a synonym for the people of Jerusaelm as a community, is born in pain. And God answered the cries of the people with this question: "Shall I bring to the point of birth and not deliver?" (Is 66:9). Therefore the sufferings of the righteous community indicates the birthpangs of the new messianic age.

Birthpangs point beyond themselves. Just as maternal joy presupposes pain, so the hope of the fulfillment of God's promises presupposes pain because of the contradiction between the world as it is and the world as it shall be. The hope of Israel was certain: just as God delivers them from the natural womb, so God will deliver them from this suffering and death.

The writings of the Qumran Community, Ethiopic Enoch, and 4 Esdras all indicate that the period just prior to and including Paul's own, was filled with the strong belief that the pressures under which Israel lived were a prelude to the messianic age. The same thing appears in some of the rabbinic writings of the period. It is therefore obvious that Paul is a child of his own age, and that he is not breaking new ground with his language about the groanings of both persons and the universe. Not only the universe, writes Paul, "but even we, to whom the Spirit is given as firstfruits of the harvest to come, are groaning inwardly while we wait for God to make us sons and daughters and set our whole bodies free" (8:23).

The "harvest to come" refers to the final time when the results of human action will be taken into account. What is sown will be reaped. It also refers to the image of the "judgment" which God will exercise over the nations. This concept developed through the years, beginning with a judgment that was completed as each day passed to a judgment that was in the distant future.

> In the course of this development one can discern the influence of Persian and Hellenistic religion as well as the development of apocalyptic. Paul shifts the emphasis on the "world to come" to the present. He believes that the judgment of salvation has already taken place in Christ. While one can still separate himself from the community and from Christ, as long as one remains in the community, the "new law" will be salvation for him.[2]

While the Old Testament concept of justice (*sdq*) is rooted in interpersonal relationships, it finds its highest symbol in Yahweh's deliverance from Egyptian slavery. Through the covenant and later through the prophets, a just society was made possible which sought to protect the poor and the oppressed and at the same time established Yahweh as the champion of justice. The prophets were quick and bold to proclaim that a life lived in disregard of the poor and oppressed is a sin against God who is the one who establishes justice through his gracious acts on Israel's behalf.

In line with the thoughts of Polish biblical scholar Langkammer, Sanders maintains that for Paul, "salvation by grace is not incompatible with punishment and reward for deeds."[3] As in the best of Judaism, good deeds do not earn salvation but are rather the condition of remaining in the community:

> Paul's assurance of salvation was not assurance that his work was perfect nor that at the judgment nothing would be revealed against him for which he could be punished. In all of this, Paul's view is typically Jewish.... The distinction between being *judged on the basis of deeds* and punished or rewarded at the judgment (or in this life), on the one hand, and being *saved by God's gracious election*, on the other, was the general view in Rabbinic literature.[4]

Then Paul goes on to answer the question that the Christian Church has posed since its beginning. It deals with the exclusiveness of the church's claim concerning the coming of the messianic age: If Jesus was the messiah, why have things *not* happened which were promised such as peace, justice, and the universal worship of the one true God? This is a question which Christians have historically ignored except by spiritualizing the promises. Yet, the question is *properly* asked of those who proclaim Jesus as messiah.

In the years surrounding the beginning of the common era, there were several interpretations of the messianic hope. Some of them were quite spiritualized. But Paul's reference is not one of them, at least not completely. He refers to a concrete state in the near future in which the entire universe would find its fulfillment. And so the question stands. For Paul the answer was in the second coming of the messiah as Son of Man:

> When Jesus would return in glory, then God would fully reveal him as Messiah, Lord, and Son of Man. This outlook would have required very little change in the standard Jewish expectations about the coming of the Messiah, except that Christians would have worked out a thesis of two comings, with the second constituting the moment of final victory, of the subjugation of God's enemies, and of universal peace and abundance.[5]

The Christian answer, then, is that the Christ would return to do what Judaism had expected to be accomplished in the first appearing. Because of this, Paul writes,

> We have been saved, *though only in hope*. Now to see is no longer to hope: Why should a man endure and wait for what

he already sees? But if we hope for something we do not yet
see, then, in waiting for it, we show our endurance (8:24-25).

To those who doubt and waiver, Paul's urging to consider "the
sufferings of this present time" as not worth comparing to what is
going to happen, was not quite convincing. They reasoned: "If sin
were as deeply rooted in the flesh as had been argued, on what
grounds could they hope for its defeat? Must they not be able to see
clear evidences of the redemption of 'our bodies'"?[6] Paul tries to encourage them in hope and bases that hope on the resurrection of
Jesus Christ.

In urging hope, Paul is not proposing a consoling dream but a
trust and patient waiting on something that is sure and based, not
on clearly seen or tangible evidence, but on the past faithfulness of
God. Our hope is in God alone, says Paul, who will do for the
whole of humanity what has been promised. How it will happen or
when it will happen is not the most important question. It will
happen in God's time and in God's way.

Because of this hope in God's faithfulness, we have the ability
to endure as we wait for this promised divine liberating activity.
One of the highest examples of endurance in Jewish literature was
Job who continued in hope even though he could see no basis for
that hope. Such endurance does not arise from a passive or stoic in-
sensitivity, but from the vitality of the Spirit which is ours from
God. Now that we are all justified through faith in God, we can all
live in hope.

We groan inwardly while we wait the full coming of God.
Indeed, our groans are so deep that we do not even realize they are
present. Yet, writes Paul,

> In the same way the Spirit comes to the aid of our weakness.
> We do not even know how we ought to pray (or, what it is
> right to pray for), but through our inarticulate groans the
> Spirit himself is pleading for us, and God who searches our in-
> most being knows what the Spirit means, because he pleads for
> God's people in God's own way; and in everything, as we
> know, he cooperates for good with those who love God and are
> called according to his purpose (8:26-28).

The Spirit is the conscience of God acting on our behalf. This reference is not to glossolalia, or speaking in tongues, but rather to the

subconscious desire of our beings to reach out to God. As Viktor Frankl explains, there is an unconscious religiousness inherent in all persons which is to be understood as "a latent relation to transcendence."[7] That relationship at its deepest level must be unconscious — "unconscious in the sense of being unreflectable."[8] We do not even know how to pray for this deepest of all desires, but the Spirit pleads on our behalf. God has thereby supplied the means of our prayer even when we do not know how to pray. In this way, God is again seen as faithful in "cooperating for good with those who love" God and are open to the divine movement that is within them.

God is also shown to be faithful since we receive the divine call even before we have a chance to prove ourselves. This is often referred to as foreknowledge or predestination. Just as God called Israel into being as the people of God, so now God calls the Gentiles to be a part of that family. The *Jerusalem Bible* puts it this way:

> They are the ones he chose specifically long ago and intended to become true images of the Son, so that his Son might be the eldest of many brothers. He calls those he intended for this: those he called he justified, and with those he justified he shared his glory (8:29–30).

Because of the transcendent character of the Christ, that is, the creative activity of God, it is not too much to suggest here that Paul is referring to Israel as the true image or model as the Son of God. Israel, as the Son of God, had been chosen to be the "eldest among a large family of brothers," thereby witnessing to the universal aspect of God's family. This, then, was the purpose for which God called Israel. Having called Israel, God justified Israel. With those he justified, he shared his glory. Thus God says through Isaiah's witness: "I will grant deliverance in Zion and give my glory to Israel" (46:13).

Beginning where the doubting and wavering ones were, Paul speaks of the election of Israel and its universal destiny. Having shown how the Spirit intercedes on the behalf of all, he goes on to assure them of the eternal or "pre-ordained" purpose of God to glorify all of those who are thereby called.

Sandmel is instructive when we consider this pre-ordaining activity of God. The term he prefers to use is "providence." The Hebrew term that is an equivalent is *tzofe*, "see," or "God sees." Providence

never concluded that a totally unalterable future lay ahead, for
such a view contradicted God's omnipotence and mercy. Nor did
the view that God fixed a man's destiny eliminate either man's
free will or his moral responsibility; if, philosophically, a doctrine of providence and a doctrine of free will and moral responsibility seem contradictory (as, when carried to extremes,
they are), Jewish thought never so extended either doctrine to
preclude the other.... Unless God's proposed destiny for a man
is subject to alteration, prayer to God to institute such alteration is nonsensical.[9]

Thus, election and free will are two sides of the same coin in
Judaism. Paul's message, then, is that all have been called, all have
been pre-ordained for justification. And if all have been called, and
all have been justified, then all will share equally in the glory of
God.

With that, Paul begins to build the majestic strains of his sym-
phony. God's universal intention for humanity is effective in every
situation. Therefore — and the words almost shout from the printed
page: "If God is for us, who is against us?" Are some condemned
because they no longer follow the ritual and the law? Are some
condemned because they continue to follow the ritual and the law?
To those who waver between the two options, Paul says that God
gave Christ up for us *all*, so that because of that self-giving of
Christ we know that there can no longer be any distinction: "...with
this gift in mind, how can God fail to lavish upon us all he has to
give?" Then Paul strikes the chord at the heart of his argument:

NEB	*NEB footnote*
Who will be the accuser of God's chosen ones? It is God who pronounces acquittal; then who can condemn? It is Christ — Christ who died, and, more than that, was raised from the dead — who is at God's right hand, and indeed pleads our cause.	*Who* will be the accuser of God's chosen ones? Will it be God himself? No, he it is who pronounces acquittal. Who will be the judge to condemn? Will it be Christ — he who died, and, more than that, was raised from the dead — who is at God's right hand? No, he it is who pleads our cause.

Minear explains why this particular form of argument was especially important in Paul's progression:

Such a mode of argument was designed to be most germane not to self-assured partisans but to diffident and uncertain waverers whose faith was subject to attacks from both sides, whose trust was not kept between themselves and God (14:22), so that their behaviour did not proceed from faith.[10]

If God has pronounced acquittal, and Christ does not judge us but rather pleads our cause,

then *what* can separate us from the love of Christ? Can persecution, hunger, nakedness, peril, or the sword...? in spite of all, overwhelming victory is ours through him who loved us. For I am convinced that there is nothing in death or life, in the realm of spirits or superhuman forces, in the world as it is or the world as it shall be, in the forces of the universe, in heights or depths — *nothing in all creation that can separate us from the love of God in Christ Jesus our Lord* (8:35–39).

Despite the internal and external sufferings of these faithful of God who waver, they can face the future with confidence that they "are more than conquerors through him who loved us."

17

The Justice of God

In Romans 9–11 Paul moves into the critical area of defending himself against charges which either have arisen or he anticipates as certain to appear. The *New English Bible* uses "The Purpose of God in History" for the heading of this section, while Minear refers to them as "The Eternal Triangle: Rebuttal." Minear sees the following issues as arising from those who must deal with Paul's gospel. The charges:

> When this apostle claims to love his Jewish kinsmen, he is a liar (9:1f). He has completely cut himself off from his own brothers and deserves to be accursed (v.3). He has become a traitor to them, by denying openly the validity of their call, the covenants, the Law, the worship, the the promises (v.4). He has portrayed the patriarchs and ignored the fact that Jesus came as the Messiah of Israel (v.5). He has gone over to the Gentiles because he believes that "the word of God has failed" (v.6). He even contends that many Jews are bogus and that many uncircumcised Gentiles are authentic sons of Abraham (v.8). He has no desire to save Jews and makes no attempt to do so; but instead he continues to antagonize members of the synagogue (10:1). According to his gospel God has rejected Israel and accepted Israel's age-long enemies. If this were true, God would be terribly unjust. He would be taking no account of Israel's sacrifices through the centuries but would be treating the Pharoah as if he were as good as Moses (v.17). Paul claims openly that God has rejected his people because of their sins (11:1), even though logically God should find no fault with them, inasmuch as he gives his mercy to whatever nation he

wishes without respect to merit. The worst Gentiles have a right to salvation, whereas the most faithful Jews have lost that right.[1]

Thus the charges against Paul, either real or apparent, are stated. He will accept some as true and deny others as clearly false. This is an essential section in our understanding of Paul. As I have worked with scores of seminary students as they prepare for United Methodist ordination, I have found a high proportion of them holding to ideas which Paul herein denies. Therefore, there is a continuing need for the church to restate the position Paul maintains in these chapters.

We should remember that Paul is still addressing primarily those Christian Jews and Gentile Christians who waver and doubt which way to go; those who are kept in confusion by the arguments of both sides. In this section we hear echoes of the rabbinic formula, "this *and* that."

Have God's purposes been frustrated by the Jewish doubt that Jesus is the long-awaited messiah? If there is a distinction between the totality of Israel and the Israel of faith, what happens to the promises of God which imply the totality of Israel? Has God's mind changed concerning the promises of Israel? And if so, is God therefore unjust and unfair?

It is highly probable that Paul had met these questions all along the way of his ministry. It is even more probable that these charges came from the opposing camps in the congregations such as in Corinth where rival groups debated Paul's message.

> The party of Cephas would presumably be that of "judaizers," advocates of observing the mitzvot. Apollos is identified in Acts 18:24-28 as a Jew of Alexandria, and possibly the "party of" Apollos was extremely partisan to allegory, as was Philo, and possibly espoused a contrast beyond that of Paul between "flesh" and spirit, and possibly was unconcerned about the literal traditions taught about Jesus. Possibly, the "party of Christ" was even more extreme.[2]

Sanders points out that the struggle in Paul is between a Jewish emphasis on "covenantal nomism" (salvation by election) on the one hand, and on the other an emphasis on "participationist eschatology" (salvation by being in Christ). For Jewish/Christian relations, the issue is one of emphasis rather than one group being superior to the other. But, writes Sanders, "Paul's view could hardly be maintained, and it was not maintained. Christianity rapidly became a new covenantal nomism...."[3]

The personal struggle in Paul between these emphases undoubtedly led to the charges against him. His own style of wrestling with the issues raised questions in the minds of his hearers and brought about a certain amount of confusion. The early church had its own criticism of his writings. While realizing that he was often misinterpreted, they found him difficult to understand. Stendahl maintains that Paul was an intellectual theologian among operators! In Second Peter we read:

> Bear in mind that our Lord's patience with us is our salvation, as Paul, our friend and brother, said when he wrote to you with his inspired wisdom. And so he does in all his other letters, whenever he speaks of this subject [of awaiting the new heavens and a new earth], *though they contain some obscure passages*, which the ignorant and unstable misinterpret to their own ruin, as they do the other scriptures (or his other writings) (3:15–16).

Paul was honored but not understood by his own followers. The reference in Second Peter speaks to those who doubt, since the "unstable" refers to those who are unsettled, uncertain, or double-minded. Paul refers to them as the weak in faith. It is this group who were most vulnerable to Paul's attackers. For the sake of these weaker brothers and sisters, Paul answers their charges.

This ninth chapter continues the issue raised in chapter eight. What can the Law do and what can it not do? How have the just requirements of the Law been fulfilled in Christ Jesus?

As a prelude to his argument that "not all descendants of Israel are truly Israel, nor, because they are Abraham's offspring, are they all his true children" (9:7), Paul states his affirmation of Israel and his love for his fellow-Jews:

> For I could even pray to be outcast from Christ myself for the sake of my brothers, my natural kinsfolk. They are Israelites: they were made God's sons; theirs is the splendour of the divine presence, theirs the covenants, the laws, the temple worship, and the promises. Theirs are the patriarchs, and from them, in

natural descent, sprang the Messiah. May God, supreme above
all, be blessed forever! (9:4-5).

"Would you be willing to have your soul damned to hell for the
salvation of another person?" That question is attributed to John
Calvin who saw in its answer the supreme test of Christian Love.

Using Exodus 32:9-14, 31-32 as the basis of a Moses typology,
Clark Williamson points to the test of a true archetypal figure:

> And the Lord said to Moses, "I have seen this people, and be-
> hold, it is a stiff-necked people; now therefore let me alone,
> that my wrath may burn hot against them and I may consume
> them; but of you I will make a great nation."
>
> So Moses returned to the Lord and said, "Alas, this people
> have sinned a great sin; they have made for themselves gods of
> gold. But now, if thou wilt forgive their sin — and *if not, blot
> me, I pray thee, out of thy book* which thou hast written."

J. Gerald Janzen comments on this passage:

> Moses was unwilling to accept an offer of founding a new
> people of God, a status which would first be withdrawn from a
> people unto whom it once had been given by an oath. Not
> only that, but he so identified himself with that people, that, in
> his intercession, he would rather that he himself be blotted out
> from Yahweh's book than that they go unforgiven.[4]

In 9:3, Paul says much the same thing, although without the passion or flair of Moses. The question posed by Williamson and
Janzen to those Christians among us who claim that Christianity
has displaced Judaism is: "Who is the more efficacious mediator/
intercessor? Who is the archetypal figure, and who the shadowy
and imperfect approximation to that figure?"[5] Christians who argue
that Christianity has displaced Judaism thereby deny the faithfulness of God's witness through Jesus and set up a weak and idolatrous substitute. We must assert with Paul that Jesus stands within
the tradition of Moses and Abraham as the bearers of God's revelation to the peoples of all the earth.

"Would you be willing to have your soul damned for the salvation of another person?" Here Paul is put to the test and he answers:
"I could even pray to be outcast from Christ myself for the sake of

my brothers and sisters. Now, do these brothers and sisters for whom he is willing to sacrifice himself represent all Jews? No, Paul answers emphatically in these first thirteen verses of chapter nine; only those who do not hold faith in God as did Father Abraham.

Paul's entire argument rests on the assumption that God's promises cannot and will not be proven false. Therefore, he refers back to the story of Abraham's and Sarah's child, Isaac (Gen 18:9-15, 21:1-13). It is not all of Abraham's children who are to be the chosen of God, but only those of Isaac's line. Ishmael did not carry on the line of Abraham. Now, says Paul, Isaac was not just any child — he was a child of promise, a miracle of old age. Because of this, "the principle of promise, rather than natural genealogy, was introduced into the Jewish race from the start."[6]

At this point Paul's argument is on shaky ground, since Ishmael was born to Sarah's slave, Hagar. This could have raised the issue of free-born versus slave-born. Therefore, Paul hastens to his back-up evidence. Isaac and Rebekah had twins, yet only one of them is regarded as a patriarch (Gen 25:19-26). Here Paul rests his case, having demonstrated through Esau and Jacob that God's promise is not one of heredity, but of selection. And because it rests upon God's selection, it could not be based on one's deeds. The choice was made prior to birth (Gen 25:23).

But does this illustration mean that "God [is] to be charged with injustice?" (9:14). Is God's pre-determining capricious?

> By no means! For God says to Moses, "Where I show mercy, I will show mercy, and where I pitty, I will pity." Thus it does not depend on man's will or effort, but on God's mercy.... He not only shows mercy as he chooses, but also makes men stubborn as he chooses (9:14-18).

This is essential to Paul's later argument where he will say that "this partial blindness has come upon Israel *only until* the Gentiles have been admitted in full strength" (11:25; 11:7).

Paul has now painted himself into a corner. Refusing to deal with the injustice of God in this situation, he takes advantage of those he seeks to help and overpowers them with the question:

> Who are you, sir, to answer God back? Can the pot speak to the potter and say, "Why did you make me like this?" Surely the potter can do what he likes with the clay. Is he not free to make

out of the same lump two vessels, one to be treasured, the
other for common use? (9:19–21).

Because of his argument on behalf of the salvation offered in Christ
to *all* who hold faith in God, the forms of the concept of predestination known in Christianity, especially in Calvinist Protestantism,
will not hold up. For Judaism, free will and election were not in
total opposition, but two sides of the same coin. Sandmel suggests
that the term "providence" is a more appropriate term. Providence
suggests that there is an ultimate purpose for each human life, and
that purpose is that all shall eventually come to know God and to
dwell in the divine light of God's presence. It is this high view of
God's ultimate aim for human life that led Schweitzer to view predestination as meaning that individuals have only the right to
refuse God's grace. The relationship between free will and providence is necessary for us to see, since to believe otherwise would
make prayer nonsensical. Indeed, process theology provides us a
framework which says that the future is never so determined that it
cannot change—either in the life of the individual or society.

Paul quotes the prophets in supporting his argument about the
providence of God. He writes: God can do anything he wants
simply because he is God. Therefore we should not question God.
That is Paul's way of dealing with this question. Of course, the
Bible if full of instances where God is questioned by the people, and
persons of the stature of Abraham and Moses. But it is not generally a rebuking of God. Job asked the question: "Who will ask
[God] what he does?" (9:12).

Paul's illustration of the potter and the clay is, of course, not
original with him. Both Isaiah and Jeremiah used this imagery:

How you turn things upside down,
as if the potter ranked no higher than the clay!
Shall the thing made say of its maker,
"He did not make me?"
Shall the pot say of the potter,
"He has no skill?" (Is 29:16)

Will the pot contend with the potter,
or the earthenware with the hand that shaped it?
Will the clay ask the potter what he is making?
or his handiwork say to him, "You have no skill?" (Is 45:9)

"But now, Lord, thou art our father;
we are the clay, thou the potter,
and all of us are thy handiwork." (Is 64:8)

Can I not deal with you, Israel,
says the Lord,
as the potter deals with his clay?
You are clay in my hands like the clay in his,
O house of Israel. (Jer 18:5–6)

"Such vessels are we, whom he has called from among Gentiles as
well as Jews," writes Paul. And then, quoting from the first chapter
of Hosea, he writes: "Those who were not my people I will call My
People, and the unloved nation I will call My Beloved. For in the
very place where they were told, 'you are no people of mine,' they
shall be called Sons of the living God" (Rom 9:25–26; Hosea 1:8–
10).

Paul's prooftexting shows up at this point. Rather than continuing with the verse from Hosea, he chooses another verse from
Isaiah which uses a similar imagery but goes off in a different direction:

Hosea: "The Israelites shall become countless as the sands of the
sea which can neither be measured nor numbered."

Isaiah: "Though the Israelites be countless as the sands of the
sea, only a remnant shall be saved."

This imagery of the grains of sand refers back to God's promise to
Abraham: "I will bless you abundantly and greatly multiply your
descendants until they are as numerous as the stars in the sky and
the grains of sand on the sea-shore" (Gen 22:17).

Paul's introduction of the "remnant" will come to the fore in
chapter ten. Here we need to reaffirm the significance of Paul's continuing relationship to Judaism. The issue is not between Paul and
Israel, but between Paul the Jew who understands the role of faith
in God's salvation and those brothers and sisters who mistakenly
see the role of good works as primary in God's salvation. At this
point in time it is for him an inhouse fight over whether Gentiles
can come to this salvation without the rites and observances of
Jewish temple ritual. It is a family quarrel, and not to understand

this is to misread Paul completely. To see it otherwise is to end up with the question which Dodd asked: "How on earth were Jews to know that faith is primary over works of the law, and how can they be held responsible for this error?" Paul answers this and clearly shows that it is an inhouse issue. The righteousness of God has been manifested "through the law and the prophets." Here in chapter nine Paul shows that there are two different strands of tradition concerning the law (modern scholarship distinguishes these as P and D). The P or priestly code is concerned with correct observance. Thus we read in Leviticus: "You shall therefore keep my statutes and my ordinances, by doing which a man shall live" (18:5). The D or Deuteronomic code provides a more inward interpretation of the law.

Paul is careful to substantiate his argument at every point from scripture—the authority of which the whole family agreed to in some degree. With this in hand, he writes that "from the beginning God had intended, by showing wrath towards his own people, to open the way for sharing his glory with his non-people." Again, sin forces us to see God's love as wrath. Wrath is therefore not for destruction but for the purpose of demonstrating divine righteousness. With the reference from Hosea in mind, he tried to show that God's

> desire to include a non-people among his sons had been the key to his patience with his own people (9:22-26). The process of election, as Paul understood it, was always open-ended. God's treatment of Israel had been designed all along to open the way for the accession of Gentiles. *This accession, however, did not cancel the promise to Israel.*[7]

Those who rely on faith in God for justification are made righteous because of that faith—Jew and Gentile alike. Those who rely on works for justification have missed the point of God's grace in either the covenant, the prophetic promises, or Jesus Christ. Pointing to Abraham, Paul speaks of the rock of faith. It is interesting to note that not only Simon Peter but also Abraham is spoken of as the "rock" upon which the true revelation of God is based. Isaiah called out:

> Listen to me, all who follow the right and seek the LORD:
> look to the rock from which you were hewn,

> to the quarry from which you were dug;
> look to your father Abraham
> and to [your mother] Sarah who gave you birth. (51:1-2)

Paul combines the following two verses from Isaiah to further explain why some have chosen faith while others have not:

> God shall become your "hardship," a boulder and a rock which the two houses of Israel shall run against and over which they shall stumble, a trap and a snare to those who live in Jerusalem; and many shall stumble over them, many shall fall and be broken, many shall be snared and caught (8:14-15).

and

> These are the words of the Lord God:
> Look, I am laying a stone in Zion, a block of granite,
> a precious corner-stone for a firm foundation;
> he who has faith shall not waver (28:16).

In the first, Isaiah warns the people against accepting the Assyrian way of life. But since the people have been weak and have not heeded this warning, God has become to them a stumbling block rather than a source of strength. They have relied on military might and immediate security rather than on the faithfulness of God. Paul uses this to argue that those who follow the law for salvation have relied on their own strength, on their ability to follow the law, and have in that sense abandoned faith in God's leading providence. They have relied on the immediate security of works rather than the long-range promises of faith.

The second text points to the source of true power and lasting security. God offers the people freedom from fear if they will live in faith and not try to escape through the expedient. Thus Paul concludes: "He who has faith in God will not be put to shame" (9:33).

Therefore, those who doubt and waver can find assurance that God has not changed the rules of the game in midcourse, since justification by faith has been the norm since the time of Abraham. Faith becomes a stumbling block when it meets the insistence of an exclusive understanding of election and salvation which shut everyone else out. Indeed, faith continues to be a stumbling block to this very day when Christians refuse salvation to persons of faith in other religions, or when Christians begin to rely on rite and good works to secure their justification. Thus, the message of Romans continues to be important today.

18

Christ as the End of the Law

"My deepest desire and my prayer to God is for the salvation of my brother and sister Jews." Thus, Paul continues his address to those who doubt and waver between justification by faith in God's graciousness and justification by works. Here Paul renews his concern for those who rely on works to secure their justification. For him to have included all Jews in this prayer would have been utterly presumptuous. He explains:

> To their zeal for God I can testify; but it is an ill-informed zeal. For they ignore God's way of righteousness, and try to set up their own, and therefore they have not submitted themselves to God's righteousness. For Christ ends the law and brings righteousness for everyone who has faith (10:2–4).

Or as the alternate reading of the last sentence better suggests, "Christ is the end of the law *as a way to righteousness* for everyone who has faith" (i.e., in God). God's way is that of faith, and this is the special emphasis of Christ.

It would appear that Paul is here digressing from his earlier argument by speaking as though there was a time when the law *was* a valid means of securing righteousness. This hardly coincides with his earlier argument that since Abraham, the Father of Israel, faith has been the only means whereby one is to be found righteous. However, being the diplomat that he is, Paul is saying in effect: "Alright, let us assume that there may have been a time when one could be judged righteous by works of the law. After all, Moses did write, 'The man who does this shall gain life by it.' But Moses also wrote, 'the Lord your God will circumcise your heart and the heart

130

of your offspring, so that you will love the LORD your God with all
your heart and with all your soul, that you might live.' Thus, all of
your good works issue in response to that faith which is deep
within you." Then he goes on to restate Deuteronomy 30:12–13 for
these doubters in the light of the revelation of God in Christ Jesus:

Deuteronomy	*Romans*
The *commandment* that I lay on you this day is not too difficult for you, it is not too remote.	The righteousness that comes by faith says,
It is not in heaven, that you should say, "Who will go up to heaven for us to fetch it and tell it to us, so that we can keep it?"	"Do not say to yourself, 'Who can go up to heaven?' (that is, to bring *Christ* down),
Nor is it beyond the sea, that you should say, "Who will cross the sea for us to fetch it and tell it to us so that we can keep it?"	"or 'Who can go down to the abyss?' (to bring Christ up from the dead)." But what does it say?
It is a thing very near to you, upon your lips and in your heart ready to be kept.	"The word is near you: it is upon your lips and in your heart." This means the word of faith which we proclaim.

Indeed, as we asked earlier, "Is Christ the new Torah?" The terms
appear almost interchangeable for Paul. Christ is the function of
God's revelation in the midst of humanity, just as the Torah was.
And just as Paul tells us here that the word of faith, i.e., Christ, is
near, clear, and life-giving, so Moses had said of the commandment of God. Unlike the Temple, persons may carry the Torah
with them wherever they may be because it is written upon their
hearts—it is a part of the very fabric of their lives. For Paul, the
same is true of the word of faith as revealed in Jesus Christ.

What makes this meaningful to Gentiles is the hope and faith
that in the witness of Jesus Christ God has declared the divine
intention that all persons should come under the eternal covenant.
For those doubters to whom Paul was singling out here, this meant
that Christ is a part of God's revelation just as is the Torah. The
early Christian communities developed the confessional phrase,
"Jesus is Lord," in order to achieve this perspective. To those who
were wavering, Paul says that salvation is to be found in the faith
which one holds in God, and that this faith is exemplified in the
phrase which many were already using:

> If on your lips is the confession, "Jesus is Lord," and in your
> heart *the faith that God* raised him from the dead, then you will
> find salvation. For the faith that leads to righteousness is in the
> heart, and the confession that leads to salvation is upon the lips
> (10:9–10).

Faith is not mere belief or verbal confession, but an attitude of
life that determines all of what we are and do. Paul is asking his
readers to live in terms of the already accepted formula confession,
Jesus is Lord." That is, in the witness of Jesus Christ we see God
active as redeeming righteousness and calling all persons to partici-
pate in the divine life through faith. But we must be cautioned once
again, it is not what *Jesus* has done but what *God* has done and is
doing.

How are we to maintain that Paul remains within Judaism and
at the same time support this call for confession that "Jesus is Lord"?
Twenty centuries of Christianity have maintained that it is this confession that distinguishes Christianity from Judaism, that separates
the parent and the child. Christians have killed, maimed, slaugh-
tered, abused and discriminated against Jews in order to preserve
this distinction. Jews, on the other hand, have accused the church
(often rightly) of breaking the first and most important commandment by substituting a bi-theism for monotheism.

I doubt that Paul saw the lines as clearly drawn as either Christians or Jews have supposed, although both have some justification
from their historical perspectives. It was this affirmation which,
after the destruction of the Temple, divided Christians from the
parent body. It was this phrase interpreted literally that led to the
charge against Christians that they were idolatrous since they
worshiped two gods.

We need to remind ourselves at this point that Paul shows little
or no concern for the historical Jesus. The importance of Jesus lay
in the function of God's revelation which we have seen in him.
Therefore, the form was not as important as the function, although
the function cannot operate without some form for expression.
Willi Marxsen explains:

> ...the Christ kerygma involved statements of function. This is
> expressed in particular in the many statements: what happened
> in the past happened "for us." The "titles" of Jesus must also be
> understood in this way. For example, there was no intention of

saying that Jesus was demonstrably and recognizably "the Messiah," but rather that he must be understood in connection with the functions of the Messiah. Conceptions known from late Judaism and apocalypticism were not uncritically transferred to Jesus. On the contrary, the functions which are encountered in Jesus determine what are to be regarded as messianic functions. It now no longer makes sense to await a Messiah, unless this would mean awaiting Jesus the Messiah who has been exalted to God's presence, is present in the Spirit and is soon coming again.[1]

Earlier we saw how the gospel writers took the functions attributed to the great leaders of historical Judaism and applied them to Jesus. Jews living outside of the Temple influence did not find this type of "modeling" hard to understand. The Greek world prepared them for it. Thus, Paul uses the scriptural roles and applies them to Jesus, thereby coming to a description of Christ not necessarily in accord with the life of the historical Jesus.

"Jesus is Lord." Paul quotes this confession also in 1 Corinthians 12:3. To see in this an identification of Jesus with God is preposterous. Paul always refers to prayer as directed to God. Even in 2 Corinthians 12:8 Paul is concerned with the presence of Christ as a healing presence rather than any reference to the historical Jesus. For Paul, "it is not a continuous career of the earthly Jesus that is understood as the saving event, but the *sending* of the Son as such,"[2] with the emphasis being on God's action through this particular manifestation. "Jesus' person and fate do not have their significance in the perceivable character of an occurrence within this world.... Faith comes from beyond, and the Beyond towers far above this world."[3] Thus, the Son is clearly a function of the Father and therefore the Son is subordinate to the Father. To say that "Jesus is Lord" is to say that "because the Son is God's activity in relation to the world, one meets God in him...."[4]

The formula confession "Jesus is Lord," then, refers to the one who opens the way of salvation for Gentiles and for all persons of faith. To say that the way of law does not lead to salvation does not mean that Paul is destroying the law, any more than did Jesus; but it does say that faith since the time of Abraham is *prior* in terms of salvation.

Isaiah wrote: "Everyone who has faith in him [God] will be saved from shame" (28:16). And that "everyone is emphatic for Paul:

—everyone: there is no distinction between Jew and Greek,
because the same Lord is Lord of all, and is rich enough for
the need of all who invoke him. For everyone, as it says again
—"everyone who invokes the name of the Lord will be saved"
(10:11-13).

And the prophet Joel had written: "Then everyone who invokes the
Lord by name shall be saved" (2:32). Paul emphasizes this because
he wants to strengthen the faith of those who doubt and waver.
Everyone who calls upon God in sincerity of heart will be saved.
Salvation comes not by works of the Law, although they are essential for growth. In his quotes from Isaiah and Joel, and in his own
argument, Paul "defended his gospel, defended the inclusion of the
Gentiles, and defended the standing of the waverers against those
attacks from the right to which they would have been most vulnerable."[5]

But what of those who have not heard the inclusive invitation?
Most of us can remember asking that question in our younger years
as we were approaching a faith commitment. Surely, those who
have not heard cannot be held responsible for not responding to
that which they do not know! And so Paul states the issue:

How can they invoke one in whom they had no faith? And
how could they have faith in one they had never heard of? And
how hear without someone to spread the news? And how could
anyone spread the news without a commission to do so?
(10:14-15).

Now, says Paul, if the issue is one of a proper commission, "there is
evidence in Scripture (Isaiah 52:7) that those who bring *good news*
authenticate themselves (their feet are *welcome* or '*beautiful*')...."[6]
(See also Nahum 1:15.)

To continue his argument, Paul states that "faith is awakened
by the message, and the message that awakens it comes through the
word of Christ" (10:17), that is, the word proclaimed by Christ
which is the word of God. This is an important point: the message
precedes faith; and the message of God for the priority of faith
comes through the Christ-function. Because of this fact, there can
be no people who have not heard the message in some form. As the
psalmist wrote:

The heavens tell out the glory of God,
the vault of heaven reveals his handiwork.
One day speaks to another,
night with night shares its knowledge,
and this without speech or language
or sound of any voice.
Their music goes out through all the earth,
their words reach to the end of the world" (19:1-4).

Paul here returns to the theme he established in 1:19-21. No one can have been left without the message, since the word of Christ is God's own self-revelation to all peoples in various and diverse ways.

Since God's word has been revealed to all, then the issue becomes the rejection of this divine revelation. God has not rejected his people; those who strive to live without faith as their priority have rejected God. But the rejection is not complete. In chapter eleven Paul says that while many have stumbled and gotten their priorities mixed up, they have not fallen completely. No one, Jew or Gentile, is free from some degree of rejection.

As a Jew, "of the stock of Abraham, of the tribe of Benjamin," Paul continues his in-house quarrel, pointing out that many Jews do not live by the revelation of faith and grace as first demonstrated in Abraham and now in Jesus. This type of self-criticism was important for Old Testament Judaism, especially the prophets, and now to the Pharisees who sought to keep the worship of God true as well as contemporary. Paul was a Pharisee, and despite such illustrations of self-criticism as we see here, Paul never removed the Christian movement from its unity within Judaism. That issue would be left for later history.

In the same way that God promised through Elijah a "remnant" of faithful believers (1 Kings 19:9-18), God has now promised that a remnant would come into being during this difficult transition period when the Gentiles were being fully incorporated into the promises of Abraham outside the structures of ritual and "law." This takes place through grace rather than through observance of the law, since "if it is by grace, then it does not rest on deeds done, or grace would cease to be grace" (11:6).

The majority, it seems, is always enriched by the committed few. The same is true of the flow of God's purpose in human history. Indeed, as Isaiah said: "If the LORD of Hosts had not left us a

remnant, we should soon have been like Sodom, no better than
Gomorrah" (1:9; 10:20–23). The remnant is always the hope of the
future. The theme is dominant for the Hebrews; it is referred to
more than 540 times in the Old Testament alone. It speaks of what
has been called "the inherent potentiality of renewal."[7] For Paul,
this remnant consists of both Jews and Gentiles who are "selected
by the grace of God" (11:5).

Grace ceases to be grace when it is made to rely on deeds performed. Of course, this was not new. Moses had pointed this out:

> Know then that it is not because of any merit of yours that the
> LORD your God is giving you this rich land to occupy; indeed,
> you are stubborn people. Remember and never forget, how
> you angered the LORD your God in the wilderness.... (Dt
> 9:6–7).

Even in the midst of idolatry, God had given grace to Israel because
of the immensity of divine love. Now, if God has done that, will
not divine justification be extended to Gentiles who have faith?
Some of Israel have understood this inclusiveness of God's love.
These are the "select few." "The rest were made blind to the truth"
(11:7).

Then quoting Isaiah and David, Paul argues that their failure
to understand this inclusiveness does not mean the downfall of
Israel. Indeed, God has provided the means through them for
salvation to "come to the Gentiles." Because of the witness of the
Spirit of God in Jesus Christ, God sought to "stir Israel to emulation," to challenge them to excel all others in such inclusiveness.
Thus, if their slowness to learn "means the enrichment of the
world," especially "the enrichment of the Gentiles, *how much more
their coming to full strength*" will mean to the world!

In describing the failure of some Jews to understand, Paul
quotes David's prayer that God would humble those who are opposed to the divine intent (Ps 69:22). Is it a coincidence that Paul
chose to quote an incident of David's dealing with table and food to
illustrate the blindness of some Jews? Minear thinks this choice was
highly intentional:

> Why, one must ask, should Paul have selected this example
> from the many available causes of Israel's blindness? Surely
> because members of Group One [those who still follow the law]

in Rome were inclined to set the barriers of table-fellowship in
such a way as to exclude Gentile Christians. These members
were under constant pressure from the synagogue to enforce
the Torah provisions on food and they themselves exerted constant pressures on [the doubters] to do so.[8]

It should be remembered that Paul had the same problem in
Corinth. Any barriers to table-fellowship were viewed by him as an
infringement on the inclusiveness of God's grace.

By this time the Christian Jews must have been feeling somewhat put-upon by Paul, while the Gentile Christians must have
been feeling rather self-righteous. However, Paul quickly shifts his
argument to the other side, saying: "But I have something to say to
you Gentiles. *I am a missionary to the Gentiles,* and as such I give
all honour to that ministry when I try to stir emulation in the men
of my own race, and so to save some of them" (11:13–14).

Paul's ministry, then, included a witness to his fellow-Jews to
accept the principle established centuries before of God's inclusiveness as primary over all other things. He hoped that those who
doubt would accept this witness and not be intimidated by those
who insist on the law. Minear's discussion is again instructive. The
primacy of inclusiveness breaks down *all* walls of separation.

> God's objective of including the Gentiles had been realized
> through the faith of the remnant and the unfaith of the majority
> of Israel (anti-Gentilism is thus for ever eliminated from
> Israel's covenant-relationship). God's objective of securing the
> full inclusion of Israel would be realized through the faith of the
> Gentiles and even through the jealous anger on the part of
> Israel (anti-Semitism is thus forever ejected from the gospel).[9]

"Through Jesus, Israel's mission is extended to the Gentiles, but the
election of Israel is not thereby negated. It is still the center from
which the mission flows."[10] Again, we must deny that "in order to
share the election, Jews themselves must be converted to faith in
Jesus as the Christ. This is the pathway to election for gentiles, but
for Jews their original election stands."[11]

19

Universal Salvation and Election

How inclusive is the salvation of God? Does it include only Jews, or only Christians, or only Jews and Christians?

Turning his attention to the strong in faith who condemn the weak, Paul begins: "Now I am speaking to you Gentiles" (11:13). Seeking to counter the anti-Judaism among these new converts, Paul points to the obvious implication of the law in Leviticus 23:10: "If the first portion of dough is consecrated, so is the whole lump." If Israel is made holy by God, then, because Israel represents the whole of humanity, all humanity is therefore justified. Many of the new Gentile Christians did not understand the inclusive nature of God and therefore scorned those who still abided by the law. They wanted to claim the promises of God as their own exclusive right, a problem that still exists in the church to this very day. So in effect Paul says:

> If Gentiles accept him [God], they must share his love for Israel, for he took seriously "the eternal triangle" of forces as defining his vocation. Gentile believers were obligated by their own faith, so strong in their own eyes, to consider as holy both the first-fruits (Jewish believers) and the whole lump as well (Israel as a whole, both believers and unbelievers). The measure of a strong Gentile faith would be whether the believer hoped for the salvation of all branches of this tree whose root was holy (11:13–16).[1]

To demonstrate that this test of faith stands on firm ground, Paul used the illustration of the olive tree and its ingrafted wild branches (11:16–24). This image was an age-old symbol of Judaism as a family unit. The olive tree provides a symbol of strength and continuity. The tree was used for so many things that it touched almost every phase of Jewish life. The tree could endure frequent droughts and would produce for hundreds of years. It was therefore a symbol of life, as well as peace and friendship.

Paul took this well-established symbol to explain to Gentile Christians the nature of their relationship to Judaism, saying: "Remember that it is not you who sustain the root: *the root sustains you!*" (11:18). Through the grace of God, Gentiles have been made what might be called honorary Jews—honorary because Christians, and Gentiles generally, have not had to bear the history of scorn and exile as have Jews. The Christian, then, is "the pagan who, in the unaccountable mercy of God, is permitted to become a kind of Jew." In fact, "apart from Israel, which means among other things the covenant of promise, the gentiles remain on the outside."[2] Paul puts the issue in these terms in order that Gentile Christians would in no way feel superior to Jews. It also demonstrated that the covenant and promise of which Gentile Christians are recipients are one and the same as that received by Jews.

The olive tree stands as the oldest symbol depicting the strength and fruitfulness of Judaism. Israel is God's olive tree (Ps 52:8; Jer 11:16). The root and the life-giving sap represents Israel as a whole, including the heritage of the patriarchs. There is a special holiness in Israel that none can deny and none can take away. It is a holiness which Paul understood to be eternal. And because the root is holy, so also are the branches.

Some of the branches, though, have fallen off. But these will not be lost forever. Furthermore, branches from a wild olive tree have been grafted in where *some* of the original branches, *some* Jews, have fallen off through lack of faith. But there is an added significance which speaks of the mysterious working of God: the grafting ought to naturally be the other way around; and further, branches once fallen off are put back on by God, which is naturally impossible. Theologically, however, this illustrates Paul's intent: it is precisely that which seems wrong or unnatural that is now taking place through the mystery of God's faithfulness and graciousness. But the greatest mystery of all is Paul's conclusion in 11:25–26 that all will eventually be saved—Jew and Gentile alike! Thus, none is ever superior over another, but all are included in the unsearchable riches of the grace of God in Christ.

Christians, therefore, have absolutely no basis for boasting.

Nor can they assume that they can be totally independent of Judaism (11:18). The relationship is asymetrical – that is, Christians cannot define themselves apart from Judaism, although Jews do not need Christians in their own self-definition. We are to conclude, then, that in God's plan there is to be a co-existence between Jews and Christians in the unity of faith. For Paul – and more importantly, for us today – the divine community of salvation is made up at least of Jews who hold faith in God as did Abraham, and Christians who hold faith in God as did Jesus.

It may appear for a while that Jews are treated as God's enemies. But that is only in appearance since "God's choice stands" (11:28). Or, as the writer of Numbers wrote:

> God is not mortal that he should lie,
> nor a man that he should change his mind.
> Has he not spoken, and will he not make it good?
> What he has proclaimed, he will surely fulfill (23:19).

Jews are still the chosen people of God, and we Christians dare not forget that fact! As Paul says, "For the gracious gifts of God and his calling are irrevocable" (11:29). God is not fickle! God's promises are sure! The promises of inclusiveness were refused by many of the people, and so God chose to reveal the promises again through Jesus Christ.

> One side's disobedience had been the means of the other side's redemption; the other side's redemption would become the means of the first side's return. Thus, there would be none who had not been disobedient, none who had not been recipients of mercy.[3]

There is a deep mystery in this kindness of God's mercy which can only be understood in the total perspective of history. Again, Paul writes: "So that you may not be complacent about your own discernment," you Gentiles need to understand that God will eventually bring not only the full inclusion of all Gentiles into this saving grace but all of Israel as well (11:25). The sins of all will be forgiven.

Paul's argument about the mystery of God's grace leads him to a conclusion which has always been the bane of Christian exclusivism: eventual universal salvation. Since it is a mystery, we do not know what this "universal" may mean, but we do know that this salvation will be received on the basis of faith in God's grace and a faithfulness to God's will. "As in Adam all have sinned, so in Christ shall all be made alive!"

> O depth of wealth, wisdom, and knowledge in God! How unsearchable his judgments, how untraceable his ways! Who knows the mind of the Lord? Who has been his counsellor? Who has ever made a gift to him, to receive a gift in return? *Source, Guide, and Goal of all that is* — to him be glory for ever! Amen (11:33–36).

Minear suggests that the dialectical process of Paul's argument can be summarized in the following manner:

> The gentiles are idolaters:
> therefore,
> God will judge them.

> The Jews are idolaters in their judging:
> therefore,
> God will judge them.

> Since both gentiles and Jews are idolaters:
> therefore,
> God will impartially judge both.

> Since gentiles and Jews together constitute the meaning of
>   humanity:
> therefore,
> all persons will be judged before God.

> **THEREFORE:**

> We are *all* idolaters and thus under the judgment of God.
> We are all justified by God and thus the children of God.

> As in Adam *all* die, so in Christ shall *all* be made alive.

> Under the law, all were judged sinners, but Jews were justified.
> Under Christ, although all are sinners, all are justified.

Does this mean that everyone will eventually be saved? And if so, what is there to fear in the judgment to come? Indeed, as Paul's hecklers confronted him: "But if through my falsehood God's truthfulness abounds to his glory, why am I still being condemned as a sinner? And why not do evil that good may come — as some people slanderously charge us with saying?" (3:8). Obviously, Paul is not arguing that there is no judgment. Rather, his argument is that God has justified all. One need only accept this fact. He believes that once having accepted such an overwhelming gift of grace, one's new relationship would naturally produce moral behavior. But, cautions Paul — and Wesley would later make this one of his themes — the deed has nothing to do with the justification. The deed is a response — not a cause.

The issue of universal salvation is something that only a gracious God can decide, and we can state the case for it only from a stance of faith in the all-inclusiveness of the divine love. But even having stated this does not remove the reality that everyone, including the wicked, must suffer the consequences of sin. Sanders explains that for Paul, salvation by grace is not incompatible with judgment:

> Paul's assurance of salvation was not assurance that his work was perfect nor that at the judgment nothing would be revealed against him for which he could be punished. In all of this, Paul's view is typically Jewish.... The distinction between being *judged on the basis of deeds* and punished or rewarded at the judgment (or in this life), on the one hand, and being *saved by God's gracious election*, on the other, was the general view in Rabbinic literature.[4]

Thus, in good Jewish style and outlook, Paul maintains that "good deeds are the *condition* of remaining 'in,' but they do not *earn* salvation."[5]

But we must go beyond that. With John Wesley we might conclude that every person will eventually be saved, if only at the moment of their death when all earthly security has been destroyed. At that moment one knows that God alone is worthy of worship, that God alone is the source of all meaning. It is at that moment that we have nothing to grasp except the eternal love of God.

Viktor Frankl gives us an illustration of this from his own

experience in the Nazi concentration camps. His friends and family were taken from him and burned in the furnaces. As they had entered the camp, they were quickly stripped nude, so that in their nakedness even their dignity was destroyed. After a time of trying to grasp hold of various things, including service to others, he turned to his writing as a source of hope and meaning. After spending several months on the manuscript—it had literally become his life—it was destroyed by a Nazi guard. As Frankl stood there watching that manuscript go up in flames, he was empty and without purpose. It was then that he realized there is nothing on which one can ultimately rely except God.

Most of us do not come to such a deep awareness of our dependence upon God without such real crises. Wesley knew that, and it led him to affirm that in the final moments of one's life, when everything is finally stripped away, there is nothing left but God.

Can one's time run out when it will be *too late* to rely solely on the faithfulness of God? Will time run out when one can no longer say, "Just as I am without one plea?" This again is a question that must be decided by the grace of God, and our understanding of God's faithfulness to all creation will inform our thoughts about it. I can only answer that question for myself, existentially. Some may look back with deep regret at not having accepted this divine gift earlier. Regret may come at having wasted so much of life on things that are ultimately void of meaning.

But is not the basis for preaching about the shortness of life and the brevity of time precisely so that this time will not be wasted, so that it might be used to bring about God's kingdom in human society? The death in which we live when we are outside of faith can be conquered through God's gift of faith—through faith for faith. The death that surrounds us, the negative forces of life, can be overcome. We do not have to live in that death, in the life-defeating patterns of existence. With that in mind, we can hear Moses crying out to the assembled people:

> I call heaven and earth to witness against you this day, that I have set before you life and death, blessing and curse; therefore *choose life*...loving the Lord your God, obeying his voice, and cleaving to him; for *that means life to you*.... (Dt 30:19–20)

Universal salvation has always been a thorn in the side of Western religions. There is a deeply imbedded feeling that a person "ought to get what's coming to them," whether punishment or reward. Without discounting the idea of judgment, Paul weighs in on the side of *eventual* salvation for all as a part of the mystery of God's graciousness. As Karl Barth reminded us, the concept of punishment in order to satisfy the wrath of God is foreign to the New Testament. Rather, the emphasis is on "correcting love" and reconciliation. Otherwise, the triumph that persons have seen in Christ's resurrection as justifying all of humanity is less than decisive and therefore justification takes on the idea of merited grace. But in Christ we saw the involvement of God, wooing the world to himself.

For Barth, this universalism "strongly accentuates the *power*, the *abundance*, the *irresistibleness* of divine grace which does indeed meet opposition on its way but ultimately conquers every resistance."[6] This is not to disregard the seriousness of sin and guilt, but to emphasize the graciousness of God who is the Source, Guide and Goal of *all* that is." Sin and guilt cannot destroy the justification given by God. One can reject it, but that justification stands firm nonetheless. Therefore we hear the echo of Paul's words: "the gracious gift of God and his calling are irrevocable" (11:29). God's decision was made graciously in the face of both real and potential rejection. One may believe that the earth is flat, but that does not alter the fact that it is round.

There appears, then, a distinction between justification and salvation. Justification is based on the free and unmerited grace of God, while salvation is based upon a proper response to that graciousness of God. However, Paul's conclusion that all shall be saved eventually seems to indicate that death is not the end of our personal growth in righteousness. Paul does not go as far as saying this, but when his argument is pushed hard, it comes out here. In essence, Paul says to us: "The saints of God, whether Jew or Christian, whether in the militant kingdom upon this earth or the triumphant kingdom in the eternity of God's life, are to genuinely hope for the salvation of those living outside of faith in God. If this is our hope and the attitude of our life, there should be no regret if God chooses to save all humanity."

There is still the matter of justification and salvation. The fundamental premise of Judaism is that justification is the free, unmerited gift of a loving and gracious God. The proper response to this gift is repentance, forgiveness, reconciliation. The focus of this is not individual salvation, since Jews are saved by being a part of

Israel. The issue for Paul in Romans is the inclusion of Gentiles in the promises of Abraham and, as such, to include them in the salvation that is a part of the promises. As Sanders writes:

> Always, whether in Galatians or Romans, it [justification by faith] only appears where the controversy over the law has to be dealt with, and — very significantly — even then only where a Scriptural argument is to be based on the as yet uncircumcised Abraham.[7]

As in Judaism, Paul argues that Gentiles are saved through participation in the community of covenant. By sharing in that community, one dies to the power of sin and belongs to God. One stays in that community through participation in its life and ideals, i.e., good works or deeds. By "behaving correctly" one avoids punishment for misdeeds or deeds undone. In this way, "punishment *prevents* condemnation." Because of God's justification of all — through the witnesses of both Abraham and Jesus — there is assurance of salvation, although not necessarily assurance of a lack of punishment (see esp. 1 Cor 3:10–15, where Paul concludes: "If a man's building stands, he will be rewarded; if it burns, he will have to bear the loss; *and yet he will escape with his life*, as one might from a fire").

BUT AGAIN: If all are going to be saved by this gracious and loving God, why worry about justice and idolatry? There are some who will press that question, but they are among those for whom God's free gift of faith has not yet become a burning reality. They are among those who cannot yet say with Paul:

> O depth of wealth, wisdom, and knowledge in God! How unsearchable his judgments, how untraceable his ways...! Source, Guide, and Goal of all that is — to him be glory for ever! Amen.

20

Ethical Qualities for God's People

Addressing those new Gentile Christians who see no need for the Law, as well as addressing all the others indirectly, Paul points out the type of behavior that will keep them in the covenant community. Having just appealed to these Gentile Christians to see how the graciousness of God had been extended to them through the Jewish witness in Jesus Christ, he now goes on to demonstrate how they are to act toward one another:

> Gentile Christians must accept God's appointment to this role of channelling his mercy to Israel, an acceptance which would transform their attitudes towards Jewish believers. Note that this idea was at the very forefront of Paul's mind when he went on to say, "*Therefore*, by the *mercies* of God, I appeal to you, brethren...."[1]

If their lives have been truly brought under the promises of faith, then their lives must reflect that change. The hatreds and divisions in the congregations must cease. Their minds must be remade by the Spirit of God so that they will mirror the inclusiveness seen in God's faithfulness and in the witness of Jesus Christ.

> The self-assured Gentile Christians in Rome, accustomed to scoff at their Jewish colleagues, were reminded forcefully that for their worship to be appropriate...and for their action to be perfect...they must reject that conformism to this age which had been embodied in their earlier anti-Semitism.[2]

The beginning of chapter twelve is tied to the mid-fifteenth:

12:1	15:16
Therefore, my brothers, I implore you by God's mercy to offer your very selves to him: a living sacrifice, dedicated and fit for his acceptance, the worship offered by mind and heart.	His grace has made me a minister of Christ Jesus to the Gentiles; my priestly service is the preaching of the gospel of God, and it falls to me to offer the Gentiles to him as an acceptable sacrifice, consecrated by the Holy Spirit.

The footnote to 15:16 reads: "...my priestly service is the preaching of the gospel of God, so that the worship which the Gentiles offer may be an acceptable sacrifice...." By responding to the graciousness of God's mercy, Paul tells them, "you will be able to discern the will of God, and to know what is good, acceptable, and perfect" (12:2).

Freedom from the law does not mean freedom from doing those things which reflect this new relationship. We are to seek to know God's will and then to do it in an acceptable manner. In what ways, then, are these Gentile Christians to respond?

First, "adapt yourselves no longer to the pattern of this present world, but let your minds be remade and your whole nature thus transformed." To change one's mind is to have one's outlook and attitudes made different. Thus, our theology determines our behavior rather than allowing our behavior to dictate how we will think theologically.

Throughout, Paul has tried to destroy all of the barriers which have been erected between Jews and Gentiles, and between Gentile Christians and Jews. Here Paul once again attempts to demonstrate this with the illustration of all believers composing a single body through Christ's witness. Therefore, says Paul, "do not be conceited or think too highly of yourself; but think your way to a sober estimate based on the measure of faith that God has dealt to each of you" (12:3). Conceit, feeling of superiority over others, is a major block to reconciliation and to the oneness of the community. Being "one body in Christ" is a favorite image of Paul's which is not synonymous with the Church. Paul is certainly not trying to describe a new distinction between Jews and Christians, i.e., between synagogue and church, but rather he is saying that through God's gracious revelation in Christ all have been united as sons and daughters of God through faith. To say that one is better than another is to erect the barriers Christ has already broken down!

Through this body imagery we understand that we all have different functions but all are still working for the same goal. No one function of the body can claim that it does not need the rest of the body. Each depends on the others to stay alive.

"[B]ut think your way to a sober estimate *based on the measure of faith that God has dealt to each of you*." Minear suggests that this verse has "special pertinence for those who delighted in contrasting their strong faith to the weak faith of their neighbours."[3] In other words, Paul is saying to these Gentile Christians who feel superior over others:

> "The stronger your faith, the more sober should be your self-judgment." "The stronger your faith, the more transformed should you be by the mercies of God" (12:1). "The stronger your faith, the greater should be your appreciation of the grace given to others"; "The stronger your faith, the greater should be the proportion of your service to the other members" (12:4-8).[4]

Just as our functions differ, so also do our gifts and graces differ, but none is superior to the others since "they are allotted to us by God's grace" (12:6). The gifts are not our own doing, but God's. Some are given the gift of "inspired utterance"; others are given the gifts of administration, teaching, public speaking, philanthrophy, leadership, and service to others. These latter gifts are often considered secular or non-religious. But here Paul clearly says that all gifts are given by God, and since they are of God they should be employed for the benefit of the human community.

Continuing with the temptations to become conceited, Paul writes: "Love in all sincerity, loathing evil and clinging to the good. Let love for our brotherhood breed warmth of mutual affection. *Give pride of place to one another in esteem*" (12:9-10). He could not have spoken much more direct to their judgmental attitudes.

Just a few verses later (16-21) he reflects the belief that conceit is the major problem of these Gentile Christians: "Care as much about each other as about yourselves. Do not be haughty, but go about with humble folk. *Do not keep thinking how wise you are*" (16). Caring means to love with all sincerity and rejoicing in the *"one* hope according to which God will have mercy on *all*."[5] It means contributing to Jerusalem Jews in need, practicing hospitality and blessing those who condemn you and deny you fellowship in the community.

Minear draws out the special intention of Paul in verse 13 which deals with the contribution "to the needs of God's people" (or, "of the saints"). Remembering the occasion of this letter — to gather a collection for the Christian Jews in Jerusalem and to plant the seed for another collection for his mission to Spain. Further, this collection for the saints in Jerusalem was a major point at the Jerusalem Conference where the Jews under Peter's leadership approved Paul's mission to the Gentiles.

Beginning with 12:14, then, Paul was pointing out attitudes and actions which these Gentile Christians used to estrange themselves from others. Indeed, verses 9–21 are to be understood in this light, and the "evil" referred to in verses 17–21 can then be seen as a reference to the barriers that were being erected between them.

Minear sees an interesting connection between the imagery of Romans and the Corinthian letters centering around the issue of "hospitality":

> It is curious that so often in generalized teaching the apostle draws his specific examples from the area of table hospitality. Yet this is not so strange if one visualizes a situation as in 14:2f. in which dietary scruples have prevented Christian fellowship at the Lord's Table, and if we recall how significant the eucharist was to the apostles as a sacrament of unity in the body of Christ.... The same table could become the table of the Lord or the table of demons.[6]

The issue of hospitality is continued in the last section of chapter twelve, where Paul draws on the imagery of the Old Testament and the rabbinic writings. Some may feel that there is a contradiction between "do not seek revenge" (12:19) and "...you will heap live coals on his head" (12:20). The question here is: Does the code of hospitality extend also to those outside the Christian community?

Krister Stendahl has found in his study of the Qumran scrolls that at least for this community, love and hospitality are limited to the community, and that "the attitude of non-retaliation is by no means a type of love. To pursue outsiders with good is a special case of 'the eternal hatred,' not of love."[7] Because the "Day of Vengeance" will soon occur, "the proper and reasonable attitude is to forego one's own vengeance and to leave vengeance to God."[8] With this in mind, Stendahl would have us look at 12:17–21 and conclude that "the attitude of non-retaliation is motivated by the admonition to give room for God's judgment."⁹ He bases his conclusion by referring to quotations from Deuteronomy 32:35 and Proverbs 25:21. However, the imagery of "coals of fire" are not limited to these two negative aspects; Isaiah 6 is a positive example. For what we have claimed to be Paul's major concerns, it seems more reasonable to conclude that the "coals of fire" refer to the correcting love of God. In this sense it is a cleansing act. Therefore, Paul is urging them to defeat evil by responding in a manner that will be cleansing and that will at least make reconciliation possible.

21

Faith and the Political Structures

Salvation through the grace of God does not imply for Paul either the absence of good works or the freedom from social involvement. While good works do not save us, they are essential for the realization of God's Kingdom. These good works have been referred to as an "ethic of participation," through which the unity of the redeemed community and the society at large is maintained. God's gifts are given in order to be of benefit to the whole of society.

In this thirteenth chapter, perhaps the most difficult for the interpreter, Paul spells out how this ethic of participation operates in relationship to the government. For him, all authority ultimately derives from God who is the source of all power. Rulers are therefore God's agents in the world and are judged accordingly. This principle is stated in Proverbs:

> Through me kings are sovereign
> and governors make just laws.
> Through me princes act like princes,
> from me all rulers on earth derive their nobility (8:15-16).

The point is that all power derives ultimately from God, although not every government or supreme authority recognizes this. And because it may not be recognized, there is for each nation and ruler the ultimate judgment of God.

In his book, *The Politics of Jesus,* Yoder argues that the text does not claim a divine institution or ordination for *particular* governments and rulers. If this were so, the state and religion would be seen as unified. As the structures of the Christian Church developed, the church failed to maintain this distinction and as a result, rather than transforming the government, the church was transformed by it. And this captivity of the church has influenced the interpretation of this chapter ever since. Stockmeier points this out when he writes:

> Constantine completed the task of recognizing Christianity officially and integrating it into the religious and spiritual scheme of the Roman Empire. Clearly he did this in terms of his own conception. Whatever his personal experience had been, his conceptions were largely in line with Roman tradition. He accorded Christianity equal rights as a religion specifically; and *though it was a religion of a somewhat special character, it was gradually brought under submission to the state.*[1]

Paul's argument is that governments are *ordered* by God; that is, they are a part of God's plan for the ordering of the cosmos. Without government there would be chaos. If Paul appears to be calling for non-resistance to a tyrannical government — which is *not* the situation in which Paul finds himself at this particular point in time — it is only to avoid retaliation in kind. As he had written in 12:19: "Do not seek revenge, but leave a place for divine retribution," and again in 12:21, "Do not let evil conquer you, but use good to defeat evil." In a government where the people have no voice, the alternative would be violent revolution (cf. Revelation 13).

Paul is saying, in essence, that the authority of the government is not self-justifying. It is rather under the judgment of God. The authorities are "God's agents working for your good." "The authorities are in God's service and to these duties they devote their energies."

Yoder feels that this needs to be emphasized differently in order to be consistent with the rest of Paul's writings. The authorities of this world are agents of God "to the *extent*" to which they work for our good and "*when* they devote their energies to these duties." Thus, not everything done by government is necessarily good or desirable. The issue here is how we respond to the government as disciples of Jesus Christ.

Remembering that this section is directed especially to the new Gentile Christians who feel that they are strong in faith as opposed to those who are weak and rely on the law, Minear suggests that the "Gentiles were more likely to reject civil authority than were Jews.... The disrespect shown by Gentile Christians for civil authorities may have been rationalized as an expression of their new emancipation by the gospel, along with the licentiousness described in 13:13."² Since Jews were so vulnerable to persecution by Rome, Paul could have seen this disrespect as a threat to Christian Jews. Agreeing with C.D. Morrison, Minear writes: "The policy of subjection to political authority ran counter to their proud freedom and provoked a resistance to the establishment not unlike the Christian hippies today."³ This would be especially true if some of the house congregations were composed mainly of slaves who were rightly in an attitude of unrest and rebellion, although this may be reading too much of present attitude into Paul's writings.

Whether Minear and Morrison are correct on this point, it is clear that since chapters twelve and thirteen are a part of the same theme, Christian non-resistance is an expression of suffering and serving love which relies on the sense of God's triumph over evil for its strength. For Paul, this triumph is sensed to be in the near future, and to submit was not based on fear of retribution but on the hope of the swiftness of God's judgment. In this way the new congregations were able to maintain a sense of moral independence.

More than this, Paul has reflected throughout on the difference Christ makes, and how this affects *all* of creation. We can see through the witness of Christ that all of life is a gift given without distinction. All of creation is in relationship to its Creator. Through this relationship all of creation will reach fulfillment. Not only has our personal sinfulness led us to erect false gods, but beyond that in a collective manner nations and institutions have also been infected with sin so that they also fail to reflect their true natures. And what is that meaning and purpose of God for all creation? Paul speaks of it as the glorious liberty in which we are to be revealed as sons and daughters of God, and in which we shall eternally live in God. As St. Augustine put it so succinctly in his *Confessions*: "O Lord, Thou hast made us for Thyself, and our hearts are restless until they rest in Thee." *That's it.* We are made for the worship of God in which we accept all of life as a most generous and gracious gift.

Institutions and societies, then, are to reflect and make possible this relational aspect of creation. Just as in creation Adam and Eve were given charge over the earth, so all authority on earth is given by God for the perfecting of the life of all creation. Because of the Fall, the powers of death seem to have triumphed. However, through the witness of God in Christ Jesus we come to the conclusion that death does not have the final word. It cannot overcome the grace of God.

In this way, Paul joins the writer of Proverbs in claiming that all power and authority is ultimately derived from God for the purpose of an orderly creation. And because of this, he claims that "we must submit to the supreme authorities" (13:1). This is not to legitimize all political authority, since that authority is itself under the influence of sin. Since political authorities are agents of God when they devote themselves to the common good, the legitimacy of authority must therefore be defined in terms of the historical circumstances surrounding it and in the manner in which it benefits those it represents or governs.

It is therefore the obligation of the followers of Jesus Christ to support the political authorities when they are in fact working for the common good, and they are to call those authorities to account in terms of their purpose. By our righteousness, evil is shown for what it is in all its idolatrous glitter. As William Stringfellow writes in his comparison of Romans 13 and Revelation 13:

> This foolishness of the saints, this witness in the midst of defeat, is wrought in the relationship of justification and judgment, in which one who knows justification to be a gift of the Word of God is spared no aggression of the power of death but concedes no tribute to the power of death while awaiting the vindication of the Word of God in the coming of Jesus Christ in judgment.[4]

If we accept this rationale, taxes are to be paid when they support the public good and when they at least make possible for all of creation a movement in the direction of its ultimate fulfillment. And the same is true on a personal basis, regardless of who the other person is: "Leave no claim outstanding against you, except that of mutual love" (13:8). Paul again is pointing out that the judging of one another is an example of the sin of coveting, and such judgment on another's standing before God is presumptuous and idolatrous. Reflecting both scripture and tradition, Paul states that the love of neighbor is the essence of the law.

Stringfellow suggests that Paul "had so strenuous an aspiration to convert the emperor that this determined the substance of

Romans 13:1-7."[5] Paul did have an audience with Felix, Festus, and Agrippa, lesser officials of the Empire. And as he now journeys to Rome, does he indeed hope for an audience with the emperor himself? To accept this conclusion we would have to believe that the Roman officials were either a part of one of the Roman congregations or else had access to this letter, both of which are difficult to accept.

It is just as likely, and more probable, that Paul saw the time of cosmic fulfillment very near and therefore he urges Christians to hold out for just a little while longer and then the judgment of God will exact its full measure. He says as much in the next verses:

> In all this, *remember how critical the moment is*. It is time for you to wake out of sleep, *for deliverance is nearer to us now than it was when first we believed*. It is far on in the night; day is near (13:11).

Since Paul believed he was living in the "last days," he urged those who were strong in faith but weak on works to throw off their intemperate attitudes of quarreling and jealousy in order to put on the all-embracing element of loving acceptance seen in Christ Jesus. Those strong in faith who condemn the Jews who relied on following the law were prone to take their new freedom to extremes. To them, Paul writes:

> Let us behave with decency *as befits the day*: [i.e.] no revelling or drunkenness, no debauchery or vice, no quarrels or jealousies! Let Christ Jesus himself be the armour that you wear; give no more thoughts to satisfying the bodily appetites (13:13-14).

In a sense, every day is the last day, since once a moment has passed, it can never return. One of the prayers for the funeral service says it well:

> Eternal God, who commitest to us the swift and solemn trust of life: Since we know not what a day may bring forth, but only that the hour for serving thee is always present, may we wake to the instant claims of thy holy will, not waiting for tomorrow, but yielding today. Consecrate with thy presence the way our feet may go.... Lift us above unrighteous anger and mistrust into faith and hope and love by a simple and steadfast

reliance on thy sure will. In all things draw us to the mind of
Christ, that thy lost image may be traced again, and that thou
mayst own us at one with him and thee. Amen.[6]

Another interpretation of this section is offered by Arthur
Ogle. It deviates radically from traditional interpretations and will
not be readily accepted. However, since he does relate it to Paul's
directives to the Gentile Christians, we need to at least give it a
hearing.

Ogle argues that the "authorities" referred to in 13:1-7 are the
leaders of the congregations. "Although Paul does not specifically
designate the authorities as 'church' authorities any more than
'state' authorities, the Greek suggests that to be the case."[7] He goes
on to say that the Biblical usage of this particular term denoting
submission is reserved for God and the chosen leaders of God's
people. J.A.T. Robinson supports this conclusion. He writes:

> [Paul] employs the same word *diakanos* (minister) of the state
> in 13:4 as he applies within the church in 12:7; and in 13:6 he
> uses of the agents of the state the term *leiturgoi* (liturgists), cor-
> responding to the *latreia* or divine service which the church
> exists to offer (12:1). There is in fact an exact parallel with his
> own apostolate in 15:16, where he describes himself as a
> *leiturgos* of Jesus Christ in the priestly service of the gospel,
> with the Gentiles as the sacrifice he offers.[8]

If it is true that Paul is asking the Gentile Christians to submit to the
authority of these congregational leaders, there is further evidence
of their misuse of their new freedom in Christ. Ogle proposes the
following translation of these verses based on the above argument:

> Let every soul be subject to the higher authorities, for there is
> no genuine authority apart from God, and those continuing in
> God's ordination. So the ones resisting the authority have op-
> posed God's directions, and, having opposed God's authority,
> will take judgment on themselves. For the church's servant-
> leaders are not a fear to the good works (e.g., feeding hungry
> enemies 12:21) but to the evil (e.g., executing your own style of
> justice in wrath [12:20] or lying to the Holy Spirit as Ananias
> and Sapphira did [Acts 5:1-11]). If you do not want to fear the
> authority, do good and you will be praised for it.[9]

While I prefer the interpretation worked out in the earlier part of this chapter, we should leave room to explore the possibilities of this unique view.

22

Pursuing the Things
That Make for Peace

What are we to do about the differences that continue to exist among us? This is the question that Paul continues to address in chapters fourteen and fifteen. His answer is: "If a man is weak in his faith, you must accept him without attempting to settle doubtful points" (14:1). Continuing to address the strong in faith who tend to put down those who rely on ritual and works, Paul reminds them of their responsibility to each other. His counsel here reminds us of John Wesley's sermon entitled "Catholic "Spirit" (September 8, 1749), which he based on a text from 2 Kings 10:15:

> And when he was departing thence, he lighted on Jehonadab the son of Rechab coming to meet him, and he saluted him, and said to him, "Is thine heart right, as my heart is with thy heart?" And Jehonadab answered, "It is." "If it be, give me thine hand."

Here Wesley makes an important distinction between opinion and essential truth. His point, says Albert Outler,

> is that religious reality lies deeper than religious conceptuality — as evidenced by those simple but true believers whose "opinions" may be incompetent and those impeccably "orthodox" persons whose hearts nevertheless remain estranged from God and man. Opinions, then, are ways of comprehending (or miscomprehending) reality. The important thing is that reflection upon reality not be confused with reality itself.[1]

Thus, says Wesley, "Let all these smaller points stand aside. Let them never come into sight. 'If thine heart is as my heart,' if thou lovest God and all mankind, I ask no more: 'Give me thine hand.'"² In another sermon he wrote: "As to all opinions *which do not strike at the root of Christianity*, we [Methodists] think and let think."³

Trying to preserve a fragile unity between Christian Jews and Gentile Christians, Paul reiterates that God is the judge of all persons — and God has accepted those who are weak in faith as well as those who are strong (14:2–3). And if God has accepted them both, how can they not accept each other? Are they better than God? Will their pride lead them back into darkness and the ways of death?

Minear reminds us about the graveness with which Jewish Christians viewed the practice of eating the common meals with Gentiles: "It is difficult for modern Gentiles, yet necessary, to recall with what horror early Jewish Christians viewed the dangers of eating unclean meat in a Gentile city."⁴ In such a situation, "their only course of action would be to avoid all meat,"⁵ and that might be taken by the Gentile host as a snub. Therefore, says Paul, if you are as strong as you claim, you will take into account the scruples of your fellow Christians.

The same thing applies to the observance of holy days and the Sabbath. Christian Jews still observed the Sabbath as the major holy day of the week, whereas Gentile Christians viewed themselves free from the bondage of such regulations. But is one any better than the other, asks Paul?

> On such a point everyone should have reached conviction in his own mind. He who respects the day has the Lord in mind in doing so, and he who eats meat has the Lord in mind when he eats, since he gives thanks to God; and he who abstains has the Lord in mind *no less*, since he *too* gives thanks to God (14:5–6).

Thus, to the doubters, those who waver between the two sides, Paul demonstrates that both approaches are valid since God accepts both. And since we are all a part of the Body of Christ, we cannot say that we have no need of one another: "For no one of us lives, and equally no one of us dies, for himself alone. If we live, we live for the Lord; and if we die, we die for the Lord. Whether therefore we live or die, we belong to the Lord (14:7–8). Indeed, says Paul, it is for such inclusiveness that Christ Jesus died, that is, "to establish his lordship over dead and living" (14:10). There is no distinction, and therefore none is superior. We must conclude then, that we have no right to judge or condemn or hold in contempt any of our brothers or sisters, for "we shall *all* stand before God's tribunal," and "each of us will have to answer for himself." Paul's resolution is simply this: "Let us therefore cease judging one another, but rather make this simple judgment: *that no obstacle or stumbling-block be placed in a brother's way*" (14:13). Paul's argument is based on the issues of conscience and love of neighbor which in turn is based on God's faithful love as demonstrated in the lives of Abraham and especially Jesus. The argument progresses something like this:

"Nothing is impure in itself."

HOWEVER:

"If a man considers a particular thing impure, then to him it is impure."

THEREFORE:

Although nothing is impure in itself, "if your brother is outraged by what you eat, then *your conduct* is no longer guided by love."

FURTHER:

Since "the kingdom of God is not eating and drinking, *but* justice, peace, and joy, inspired by the Holy Spirit,"

THEREFORE:

You should show yourself "a servant of Christ" by not allowing what you consider allowable to become the occasion for disaster to another person.

This personal sacrifice on the part of the followers of Christ is a commitment to the work of God. Rather than picking on things that divide, "let us then pursue the things that make for peace and *build up the common life*" (14:19). If there are doubts about what is right, you must appeal to your own conscience which is informed by the love of God witnessed to in the life of Jesus Christ. Actions stemming from something other than conviction are sin. But not just any and every conviction is good, but only the conviction that stems from faith. We grow in faith daily as we strive to live in this inclusive manner. Therefore, "everything which proceeds from faith tends to produce a greater or stronger faith. Such is in fact the test of what does proceed from faith."[6]

In 15:1, Paul associates himself with those whom he calls the strong in faith, and he repeats his previous argument of 14:13ff:

> Those of us who have a robust conscience must accept as our own burden the tender scruples of weaker men, and not consider ourselves. Each of us must consider his neighbor and think what is for his good and will build up the common life.

And, of course, our model for such self-giving is Jesus Christ, "for Christ did not consider himself." Our actions are not to please ourselves or even other persons, but to please God. In that process we may please God and ourselves, while in others to please God is to make a sacrifice of self. As the Wesleyan Covenant Service prayer reminds us:

> Christ has many services to be done; some are easy, others are difficult; some bring honor, others bring reproach; some are suitable to our natural inclinations and temporal interests, others are contrary to both. In some we may please Christ and please ourselves; in others we cannot please Christ except by denying ourselves. Yet the power to do all these things is assuredly given us in Christ, who strengthens us.[7]

Glorifying God with one accord "after the manner of Jesus Christ" is the chief aim of the Christian congregations. And this unity of purpose should be evident in all that we do. "In a word," writes Paul, "accept one another as Christ accepts us, to the glory of God." Christ accepts us with our sins and failings. Indeed, he died and was raised by the power of God, so that "every knee shall bow and every tongue acknowledge God" (14:11). Individualism in Christianity is therefore always suspect. When our aim is to find satisfaction for ourselves alone, and when we forget to "build up the common life," we have denied the gospel of God.

And what was the manner of Jesus Christ in bringing glory to God? "Christ became a servant of the Jewish people *to maintain the truth of God* by making good his promises to the patriarchs, and at the same time *to give the Gentiles cause to glorify God* for his mercy (15:8–9). This statement is *absolutely essential* if we are to correctly understand Paul's mission and his message. Once again it is stated that God has not abandoned the Jews but has remained faithful to the divine promises made to the patriarchs. In the witness of Jesus Christ, then, there must be something other than just another exclusivistic religious expression. And so there is. The witness of Christ is that the Gentiles are now included in those same promises that were once given to Abraham and his descendants. These promises are not taken over by Christians, but Christians are made to share in them. This, argues Paul, is in fulfillment of scripture whereby Gentiles are foreseen as joining Israel in shouting aloud the praises of God.

Paul defies his own ministry in terms of the ministry of Jesus Christ:

> [God's] grace has made me a minister of Christ Jesus to the Gentiles; my priestly service is the preaching of the gospel of God, and it falls to me to offer the Gentiles to [God] as an acceptable sacrifice, consecrecrated by the Holy Spirit.

To Jews, Paul says that God has not limited the divine grace and mercy to them alone. To Christians, he says that neither has God limited the divine grace and mercy to them. Rather, Jew and Gentile have been united through faith in God's providence. And this we see unmistakably in the life, death, and resurrection of Jesus Christ. As a Jew, Paul's *priestly service* is to preach the gospel of God. As a Christian Jew, his specific ministerial focus was to be a minister to the Gentiles in the name of inclusive love, i.e., in the name and after the manner of Christ Jesus. "Thus in the *fellowship of Christ Jesus* I have ground for pride in the *service of God*" (15:17).

Again, lest anyone should mistakenly think that Paul is equating Jesus and God, we need to be reminded that he continually makes it clear that he is "in the service of God" in the "*manner* of Christ Jesus." While Paul elsewhere attacks pride as a form of idolatry, this pride of which he now speaks is derived from faith and points not to himself but to what God has accomplished through his life. Admittedly, there is a fine line here, even when the accomplishments are attributed to "the power of the Holy Spirit" (15:18).

Paul's style of ministry is one of innovation rather than of maintenance. He says: "It is my ambition to bring the gospel to places where the very name of Christ has not been heard, for *I do not want to build on another man's foundation*" (15:20). His call is to reach out to those who have not heard that they are now included in the grace and mercy of God and are heirs to the promises of God. That is one reason why he had not yet been to Rome. Others had been there, and besides, there was plenty of work for him to do in the area "from Jerusalem as far round as Illyricum." Paul is a pioneer. He planted the seeds of this inclusive message in the major areas of his travel. His hope was that when those seeds flourished and provided more seed and thereby began to spread on its own, then Christ would return to establish God's kingdom upon the earth. His was a mission of urgency, and if time was limited, he knew that priority must be given to the centers of significant population.

Turning to his reasons for now coming to Rome, he writes that he wants them to raise enough money to send him on to Spain. But for the moment he is on his way to Jerusalem with the collection "for the benefit of the poor among God's people at Jerusalem." This collection for Christian Jews has played an important role in Paul's mission to the Gentiles. Its purpose was to demonstrate the unity that exists between Jews and Gentiles, between the ministry of Peter and James and his own. The Christian Jews have shared their spiritual legacy with the Gentiles. Now the Gentiles are under an obligation to share their material goods with them. For this effort, Paul solicited the congregations in Rome to be his "allies in the fight":

> Pray to God for me that I may be saved from unbelievers in Judaea and that my errand to Jerusalem may find acceptance with God's people, so that by his will I may come to you in a happy frame of mind and enjoy a time of rest with you (15: 31-32).

Such a collection was not uncommon for first-century congregations. This money was particularly necessary in the more densely populated areas where persons were most likely to be without

family to provide such support, especially the widows and or-
phans. Paul's agreement to provide such aid from Gentile Christians was a sign of his solidarity with the leadership of Peter and
James. In fact, Paul was not free to go to Rome or Spain until that
obligation had been met (cf. 1 Cor 16:1; 2 Cor 8:4; 9:1; Gal 2:1-10).
From the tenor of the second letter to the Corinthians, the response
was not as strong as he had anticipated, especially after a rumor
was started that Paul and his associates were using some of the
money for their living expenses.

Here in Romans, the collection is approaching completion.
J.C. Hud tells us that this collection had several purposes. Main
among them are three:

> (a) There was genuine need, perhaps a result of property
> sharing...famine...or apocalyptic excitement.... (b) The project
> gave Paul a concrete opportunity to respond to the Jerusalem
> apostles in gratitude for their entrusting him with the Gentile
> mission.... (c) It served as a thank offering from the Gentile
> [congregations] for their share in the salvation originally given
> to Jewish Christianity.[8]

Minear points out why this collection was so strategic in Paul's
ministry by asking us to see how innovative the idea is that *Gentile*
Christians should send money to poor Christian *Jews*.

> Earlier appeals had been resisted; Paul's authority had been re-
> jected [by the Jerusalem leaders]. There were rumours that the
> whole business was graft. Unaccustomed to almsgiving, having
> few resources of their own, despising the Jews, resenting the
> ways in which Jewish Christians had opposed the Gentile mis-
> sion and [congregations], Paul's Gentile [congregations] were
> brought to open rebellion on this issue.[9]

Despite the strong opposition he faced, Paul nevertheless boldly
declared that contributing to this fund was "one of the tests of the
loyalty of the Gentile congregations."[10] This collection, "which had
estranged Gentile Christians and the delivery of which would
antagonize Jewish Christians in Jerusalem,"[11] was raised at the risk
of Paul's life. Thus, he asks for the Roman congregations' prayers
that "I may be *saved from unbelievers* in Judaea" and "my errand to
Jerusalem may *find acceptance* with God's people" (15:31).

The concluding chapter of Romans was covered at the beginning of this study, since it set the stage for the character of the congregations to which Paul was writing. Chapter sixteen shows that there were various and diverse congregations in Rome, some led by persons who had returned to Rome after being driven out only a few years earlier. It also provides a summary warning not to follow "those who stir up quarrels and lead others astray" (16:17). As a farewell ascription Paul writes:

> To [God] who has power to make your standing sure, according to the Gospel I brought you and the proclamation of Jesus Christ, according to the revelation of that divine secret kept in silence for long ages but now disclosed, and through prophetic scriptures by eternal God's command made known to all nations, to bring them to faith and obedience — to God who alone is wise, through Jesus Christ, be glory for endless ages! Amen.

We have assurance of being able to stand sure because of the gospel of God's faithfulness. This gospel has been revealed from ages past through prophetic scriptures. And although this revelation was made known in various ways to all the nations, the unifying purpose of that revelation was to bring persons to faith and obedience. The gospel of God was also revealed in the "proclamation of Jesus Christ," a proclamation of inclusiveness which has been the secret desire of God since creation.

Through both means, Jewish scripture and Christian tradition, all nations are to be brought to faith in God and obedience to the divine will. There is no longer any distinction made by God between faithful Jews and faithful Gentiles. How can we do less since we are all members of God's family! Because of the universal witness of Jesus Christ, we can all together shout aloud: "Source, Guide, and Goal of all that is — to God be glory for ever! Amen."

Conclusions

We have attempted in this study to highlight Paul's contention that the covenant which God made with Judaism has a continuing validity. The revelation of God in the witness of Jesus Christ in no way supplanted that covenant. Christianity began as a sect within Judaism, the earliest members were devout Jews who continued in the customs and rituals of the synagogue, and Christianity continued as a sect to varying degrees for almost a hundred years. Basic shifts began taking place around the time of the destruction of the Temple in 70 C.E. With these changes, the Christian sect took on more and more the elements of Greek and Roman culture until the accents of the Hebraic were largely muted.

The challenge for us today is to begin the process of an appropriate "re-Judaizing of Christianity." If we are to discover the strength of renewal and reform that was in our roots, then we must see again the universal message of salvation which Paul proclaimed. That means seeing that we are wild shoots grafted onto the well-cultivated Olive Tree which is Judaism. The basic Christian story is a Jewish reinterpretation of the religious heritage of Israel, a reinterpretation fostered in many ways by the Pharisaic tradition. Indeed, in this Pharisaic tradition we see that "Christianity had existed at least two hundred years before Jesus, its greatest and noblest spokesman, but not its originator."[1]

When Paul spoke about Jesus Christ, he understood this to be the mixture of a name and a title which were distinct and yet interrelated. Paul showed little concern for the historical Jesus. His concern was with the risen Christ. Jesus is the human form, while Christ denotes the function of God's spirit in that human form, operating to produce faith in the unfaithful, Jew and Gentile alike.

In light of this, Romans 11 must be seen to answer certain crucial questions. If the Old Testament scripture is truly the word of God and equal in authority with the tradition of the New Testament as the sufficient rule both of faith and of practice, then we are *obligated* to ask with Lasor: "(1) Is Jesus Christ the only Savior? (2) Is he the Son of God? (3) Is he the Jewish Messiah?"[2]

Now, if in fact the Old Testament is authoritative along with the New Testament, then we are forced to realize that the *process* of salvation did not begin with Jesus. Paul testified to this in Romans 4 where he proclaimed that Abraham's faith in God was the basis of his salvation. To say, then, that Jesus is "my" savior since he has revealed through his resurrection the love of God to me, is quite different from saying that Jesus is the *only* savior. If salvation is the removal of that which distorts creation, and if God is the Source, Guide, and Goal of all that is, then we are led to say with Paul that God has made that divine and saving self-revelation known at various times, in all places, and in whatever manner was most appropriate to both time and place. Salvation, then, is a story beginning at creation in the divine love of God and continues to be told to this very day. Jesus was the form of that message for his time to those outside of the covenant and to those unfaithful to the covenant. He was the form through which God's self-revelation was made clear that salvation was for *all* persons of faith.

Is Jesus Christ *the* Son of God? We have tried to show that Jesus Christ is *a* Son of God, one who was anointed with a special relationship to God for the fulfilling of a specific task. As a Son of God, Jesus claimed no privilege or status, and sought only to be a brother to all in order to bring them to the Father. This fact is generally blurred by the filtered lenses through which we view him:

> Can it be that gentile Christians have so distorted and hellenized the concept of Jesus as the Son of God that it is no longer acceptable to Jews? Or is there a mystery in the Godhead, a community of personality that required him, when he created Adam male and female (Gen. 5:1-2), a Being of such complexity that we are forced to speak of "the angel of the Lord," "the spirit of the Lord," "*bath Qol*," or "the Son of God" when we attempt to describe His redemptive activity?[3]

And what about Jesus as the Jewish Messiah? If we take seriously Paul's implied distinction between the historical Jesus and the risen or exalted Christ, we can then say that "Christians are right in asserting that Jesus is the Christ; Jews are right in asserting that Jesus is not the Messiah."[4] The terms may have been intended to represent the same thing originally, but as it passed from Hebrew to Greek, it took on a change of meaning. Interpreted in light of the spiritualization of the term by the Pharisees, it is obvious that the terms are no longer synonymous. The only similarity remaining is the hope which they represent. We can no longer say, as some groups like "Jews for Jesus" say, that in Jesus all the Jewish expectations for the coming of the Messianic Age have been fulfilled. When read in light of the prophetic background, and upon looking at the present world situation, we are forced to ask: Has the world really been radically transformed into the new earth of peace and justice?

This study has also tried to help us realize that Romans was not a doctrinal letter, but a letter addressing the very real issue of diversity and unity in the historical situation of the congregations in Rome. In our own day of continual talk of Christian unity, church union, interfaith dialogue, and an acceptance of the principle of pluralism, we need to re-read Romans as a way of dealing with the issues of the divisions that deny unity, the divergency that prohibits cooperation, the triumphalism that mars our dialogue, and the worldwide resurgence of fundamentalism that tries to defeat the principle of pluralism. We need to hear again these words in our local churches where our behavior betrays our judgmental attitude toward those who do not measure up to our standards. And we need to take another look at the importance of the collection for the poor that in a very concrete way symbolized one's commitment. How extremely important are Paul's words for us today!

Does the process of re-Judaizing Christianity mean that we are to abandon Christianity for Judaism? Is this to remove the distinctive features of Christianity that presently set it off from Judaism? The simple answer is no. What it does mean is that we must realize that in saying our own faith orientation is the *most adequate* approach in fulfilling God's will in this world is not the same as saying it is the *only* approach. Because of our faith experience, this approach has become meaningful to our lives, and it is to the God of that experience that we give witness. But in that witness it must be admitted that this by no means exhausts or limits God's realm of revelation or saving power.

Chapter Notes

Preface

1. E. Schillebeeckx, *God, the Future of Man* (London, 1969): 24.
2. Lamar Williamson, Jr., "Translations and Interpretation: New Testament," *Interpretation* 32 (April, 1978): 166.
3. *Ibid.*, p. 167.
4. L. Legrand, "The Good News Bible," *Indian Theological Studies* 14 (1977): 309–317.
5. Monica Hellwig, "Why We Still Can't Talk," *The New Catholic World* (January/February, 1974): 41.

Introduction

1. Jacob Neusner, *First Century Judaism in Crisis* (Nashville: Abingdon Press, 1975): 177.
2. Samuele Bacchiocchi, "How It Came About: From Saturday to Sunday," *Biblical Archaeology Review* 4 (September/October, 1978): 32.
3. *Ibid.*, p. 33.
4. *Ibid.*, p. 39.
5. Samuele Bacchiocchi, "Comments," *Biblical Archaeology Review* 5 (January/February, 1979): 9.
6. *Ibid.*
7. *Ibid.*
8. Bacchiocchi, "How It Came to Be," p. 39.
9. Quoted, *Ibid.*, p. 37.
10. Quoted, *Ibid.*, p. 37.
11. Samuel Sandmel, *Judaism and Christian Beginnings* (New York: Oxford University Press, 1978): 4. (JCB)
12. *Ibid.*, p. 16.
13. *Ibid.*, p. 17.
14. *Ibid.*, p. 257. See also, Lester L. Grabbe, "Orthodoxy in First Century

Judaism: What Are the Issues?" *Journal for the Study of Judaism* 8 (1977): 149–153.
15. Werner Foerster, *From the Exile to Christ* (Philadelphia: Fortress Press, 1964): 12.
16. Bruce Vawter, abstract of an article by Leo Laberge, *Old Testament Abstracts* 2 (1979): 52.
17. Foerster, p. 16.
18. H.L. Ellison, *From Babylon to Bethlehem* (Atlanta: John Knox, 1979):1.
19. *Ibid.*, p. 6.
20. See: Dan 1:1f; 2 Chr 36:10; Jer 27:16; and 2 Chr 36:18.
21. Ellison, p. 9.
22. *Ibid.*, p. 12. See also Neh 7:6–73a; 1 Esdras 5:7–46; Ezra 2.
23. *Ibid.*, p. 53.
24. *Ibid.*, p. 54.
25. *Ibid.*, p. 69.
26. *Ibid.*
27. Sandmel, JCB, p. 259.
28. *Ibid.*, p. 166.
29. James H. Charlesworth, "Focus on the Pseudepigrapha," *The Circuit Rider* 2 (September, 1968): 7–8.
30. Sandmel, JCB, p. 321.
31. Neusner, p. 38.
32. M.J. Cook, "Judaism, Hellenistic," *Interpreter's Dictionary of the Bible*, 5 vols (New York: Abingdon Press, 1962, 1976), 5:507.
33. Ellison, p. 107.
34. *Ibid.*, p. 108.
35. Cook, p. 508.
36. Samuel Sandmel, *The Genius of Paul: A Study in History* (Philadelphia: Fortress Press, 1958, 1970, 1979): 12.
37. *Ibid.*, p. 30.
38. *Ibid.*, p. 19.
39. *Ibid.*, p. 53.
40. George S. Hendry, "Theological Labels," *Theology Today* 37 (April, 1980): 72.
41. Ernest Saunders, "Christian Synagogues and Jewish Christianity in Galilee," *Explor* 3 (Winter, 1977): 70.
42. Phillip Sigal, "Unfinished Business," *Judaism* 26 (Summer, 1977): 317.
43. Ben Zion Bokser, "Religious Witness in Judaism," *Judaism* 26 (Winter, 1977): 63.
44. *Ibid.*
45. *Ibid.*, p. 64.
46. Moshe Moskowitz, "Intermarriage and the Proselyte: A Jewish View," *Judaism* 28 (Fall, 1979): 423.
47. *Ibid.*, p. 424.
48. *Ibid.* See also Neh 13:24–30; Ezra 10:1–17; Dt 7:1–3; 23:4.
49. *Ibid.*
50. *Ibid.* See Pesahim 87b.
51. Ellis Rivkin, "The Meaning of Messiah in Jewish Thought," *Union Seminary Quarterly Review* 26 (Spring, 1971): 383.

52. *Ibid.*, p. 384.
53. *Ibid.*, p. 390.
54. *Ibid.*
55. *Ibid.*, p. 393.
56. *Ibid.*
57. Ellis Rivkin, *A Hidden Revolution* (Nashville: Abingdon Press, 1978): 240.
58. *Ibid.*, p. 245.
59. *Ibid.*, p. 246.
60. *Ibid.*
61. *Ibid.*
62. *Ibid.*
63. *Ibid.*, p. 248.

Chapter 1

1. Paul S. Minear, *The Obedience of Faith* (Naperville, Ill.: Alec R. Allenson, 1971). See also Hans-Werner Bartsch, "The Historical Situation of Romans," *Encounter* 33 (Autumn, 1962): 329–339.
2. *Ibid.*, pp. 8–16.
3. Ernest Kasemann, *Perspectives on Paul* (Philadelphia: Fortress Press, 1979): 15.
4. Minear, p. 45, n.8.

Chapter 2

1. E. Earl Ellis, review of Hans-Jurgen Van der Minde, *Schrift und Tradition bei Paulus: Ihr Bedeutung und Funktion in Romerbrief, Interpretation* 31 (April, 1977): 204.
2. _____, "Saints," *Interpreter's Dictionary of the Bible*, 5 vols (New York: Abingdon Press, 1962, 1976), 4:164.
3. A.E. Harvey, *Companion to the New Testament* (New York: Oxford University Press, 1970): 421.
4. *Ibid.*
5. *Ibid.*

Chapter 3

1. William Farmer, "The Dynamics of Christianity," *Religion in Life* 38 (Winter, 1969): 576.

Chapter 4

1. Elliot N. Dorff, "God and the Holocaust," *Judaism* 26 (Winter, 1977): 33.

2. *Ibid.*, p. 33, n.18. See also Avot 4:2.
3. *Ibid.*
4. Dave Berg, *My Friend God* (New York: New American Library, 1972; "Signet Books"): 33.
5. *Ibid.*, p. 35.
6. Jon Sobrino, *Christology at the Crossroads* (Maryknoll, New York: Orbis Books, 1978).

Chapter 5

1. Alfred Jepsen, "āman," *Theological Dictionary of the Old Testament* (Grand Rapids, Mich.: William B. Eerdmans, 1974), 1:315.
2. Bokser, p. 63.
3. *Ibid.*
4. *Ibid.*, p. 64.
5. Quoted in Bokser, p. 64, italics added.
6. Quoted in Albert Nolan, *Jesus Before Christianity* (Maryknoll, N.Y.: Orbis Books, 1978): 66.
7. *Ibid.*
8. Quoted in James L. Price, "God's Righteousness Shall Prevail," *Interpretation* 28 (July, 1974): 272.
9. Joseph Haroutunian, Louise Smith, eds., *Calvin Commentaries* (Philadelphia: Westminster Press; "The Library of Christian Classics"): 224.

Chapter 6

1. Harvey, p. 508.
2. William Baird, "On Reading Romans in the Church Today," *Interpretation* 34 (January, 1980): 51.
3. Quoted in J.A.T. Robinson, *Wrestling With Romans* (Philadelphia: Westminster Press, 1979): 18.
4. Robinson, p. 19.
5. *Ibid.*, pp. 19–20.
6. *Ibid.*, p. 21.
7. Paul S. Minear, *Eyes of Faith* (St. Louis: Bethany Press, 1964): 191.
8. See also James 1:22–25; Luke 6:46–49.

Chapter 7

1. Rudolf Meyer, "Circumcision," *Theological Dictionary of the New Testament* (Grand Rapids, Mich.: William B. Eerdmans, 1967), 6:77.
2. John Wesley, Letter to Gilbert Royce, May 22, 1750.
3. Robinson, p. 34; see also Wisdom 15:1–2.

Chapter 8

1. Harvey, p. 510.
2. A. Roy Echardt, "Christians and Jews: Along a Theological Frontier," *Encounter* 40 (Spring, 1979): 112–113.
3. *Ibid.*, p. 113.
4. Calvin L. Porter, "A New Paradigm for Reading Romans: Dialogue Between Christians and Jews," *Encounter* 39 (Summer, 1978): 268–269. See also James L. Price, "God's Righteousness Shall Prevail," *Interpretation* 28 (July, 1974): 272–273.
5. Quoted in Sobrino, p. 80.
6. Sobrino, p. xxiv.
7. *Ibid.*, p. 108.
8. Raymond Abba, "The Origin and Significance of Hebrew Sacrifice," *Biblical Theology Bulletin* 7 (1977): 125.
9. *Ibid.*, pp. 123–138.
10. Robinson, p. 45.
11. *Ibid.*
12. Quoted in Buschsel, "Atonement," *Theological Dictionary of the New Testament* (Grand Rapids, Mich.: William B. Eerdmans, 1967): 3:313, n.50.
13. Buchsel, p. 313.
14. Jakob J. Petuchowski, *Heirs of the Pharisees* (New York: Basic Books, 1970): 72.
15. Robinson, p. 46.
16. *Ibid.*, p. 48.

Chapter 9

1. Minear, *Obedience of Faith*, p. 53.
2. *Ibid.*, p. 54.
3. *Ibid.*
4. *Ibid.*
5. *Ibid.*, p. 55.
6. *Ibid.*, italics added.
7. *Ibid.*

Chapter 10

1. Sandmel, *Genius*, p. 72.
2. Paul W. Meyer, "The Holy Spirit in the Pauline Letters," *Interpretation* 33 (January, 1979): 3.
3. Viktor Frankl, *The Unconscious God* (New York: Simon & Schuster, 1975): 16.
4. Minear, *Obedience of Faith*, p. 58.
5. *Ibid.*
6. *Ibid.*, p. 59.

Chapter 11

1. Max Wilcox, "'Upon the Tree'—Deut. 21:22-23 in the New Testament," *Journal of Biblical Literature* 96 (1977): 86.
2. Kasemann, p. 98.
3. George Wesley Buchanan, *Revelation and Redemption: Jewish Documents of Deliverance from the Fall of Jerusalem to the Death of Nahmanides* (Dillsboro, N.C.: Western North Carolina Press, 1978): 571-572.
4. Joseph A. Fitzmeyer, *Essays on the Semitic Background of the New Testament* (Missoula, Mont.: Scholars' Press, 1974): 57.
5. Nolan, pp. 74-75.
6. Richard L. Rubenstein, "Response to Tal's 'Jewish Self Understanding...'," *Union Seminary Quarterly Review* 26 (Summer, 1971): 368.
7. *Ibid.*
8. *Ibid.*
9. Robinson, p. 62. See also 2 Esdras 8:35.
10. Christian Duquoc, "New Approaches to Original Sin," *Cross Currents* 28 (Summer, 1978): 191.
11. *Ibid.*, p. 192.
12. *Ibid.*, p. 193.
13. *Ibid.*, p. 196.
14. Baird, p. 54.

Chapter 12

1. Hermann Samuel, Reimarus, *The Goal of Jesus and His Disciples*, trans., George Wesley Buchanan (Leiden: E.J. Brill, 1970): 68.
2. *Ibid.*, p. 70.
3. Norman Perrin, *The Resurrection According to Matthew, Mark, and Luke* (Philadelphia: Fortress Press, 1977): 83.

Chapter 13

1. Sandmel, *Genius*, p. 43.
2. *Ibid.*, p. 45.
3. Minear, *Obedience of Faith*, p. 66.
4. Schechter, p. xix.

Chapter 14

1. Minear, *Obedience of Faith*, p. 67.
2. *Ibid.*, p. 68.
3. Stendahl, p. 13.
4. George Wesley Buchanan, *To the Hebrews* (Garden City, N.Y.: Doubleday, 1972; "The Anchor Bible"): 37.

5. *Ibid.*, p. 81.
6. *Ibid.*
7. *Ibid.*, p. 107.

Chapter 15

1. Minear, *Obedience of Faith*, p. 12.
2. Sandmel, *Genius*, p. 73.
3. *Ibid.*
4. Sandmel, JCB, p. 334.
5. *Ibid.*, p. 257.
6. *Ibid.*, p. 183.
7. Quoted in Bruce Vawter's review of D.H. Odendaal, "Die Wetsgedeettes van die Ou Testament in die prediking," in *Old Testament Abstracts* 2 (February, 1979): 73.
8. *Ibid.*
9. Sandmel, JCB, p. 184.
10. *Ibid.*, p. 186.
11. E.P. Sanders, *Paul and Palestinian Judaism* (Philadelphia: Fortress Press, 1977): 420.
12. Schechter, p. 134.
13. Finkelstein, quoted in Schechter, p. xix.
14. Quoted in Schechter, p. 133.
15. Schechter, p. 131.
16. James A. Sanders, "Torah and Christ," *Interpretation* 29 (October, 1975): 374.
17. Sandmel, *Genius*, p. 51.
18. O.A. Piper, "Life," *The Interpreter's Dictionary of the Bible* (New York: Abingdon Press, 1962, 1976), 3:129.

Chapter 16

1. O.A. Piper, "Suffering," *Interpreter's Dictionary of the Bible* 5 vols (New York: Abingdon Press, 1962, 1976), 4:452.
2. Leslie J. Hoppe, abstract of article by H. Langkammer, "Koncepcja Sadu w Starym Testamencie i w Teologii Pawlowej," *Old Testament Abstracts* 2 (October, 1979): 251.
3. E.P. Sanders, p. 517.
4. *Ibid.*
5. Raymond E. Brown, *The Birth of the Messiah* (Garden City, N.Y.: Doubleday, 1977): 29n.
6. Minear, *Obedience of Faith*, p. 69.
7. Frankl, p. 61.
8. *Ibid.*, p. 32.
9. Sandmel, *Genius*, p. 226.
10. Minear, p. 70.

Chapter 17

1. Minear, *Obedience of Faith*, p. 73.
2. Sandmel, *Genius*, p. 321.
3. E.P. Sanders, p. 552.
4. Quoted in Clark M. Williamson, "The 'Adversus Judaeos' Tradition in Christian Theology," *Encounter* 39 (Summer, 1978): 295.
5. J. Jerald Janzen, quoted in Williamson, p. 295.
6. Harvey, p. 526.
7. Minear, p. 77; italics added.

Chapter 18

1. Willi Marxsen, "Christology in the NT," *The Interpreter's Dictionary of the Bible*, 5 vols (New York: Abingdon Press, 1962, 1976), 5:148–149.
2. *Ibid.*, p. 151; italics added.
3. *Ibid.*
4. *Ibid.*
5. Minear, *Obedience of Faith*, p. 78.
6. Harvey, p. 529.
7. Gerhard F. Hasel, "Remnant," *The Interpreter's Dictionary of the Bible*, 5 vols (New York: Abingdon Press, 1962, 1976): 5:735.
8. Minear, *Obedience of Faith*, pp. 78–79.
9. *Ibid.*, p. 79.
10. Rosemary Ruether, "Identities," a review of Marcus Barth's *Jesus the Jew and Israel and the Palestinians, The Christian Century* 96 (March 7, 1979): 254.
11. *Ibid.*

Chapter 19

1. Minear, *Obedience of Faith*, p. 80.
2. Eckardt, p. 112.
3. Minear, p. 80. See also the sermon by Karl Barth, "All," *Interpretation* 14 (1960): 164–169.
4. E.P. Sanders, p. 517.
5. *Ibid.*
6. G.C. Berkouwer, *The Triumph of Grace in the Theology of Karl Barth* (Grand Rapids, Mich.: William B. Eerdmans, 1956): 211.
7. E.P. Sanders, p. 438.

Chapter 20

1. Minear, *Obedience of Faith*, p. 83.
2. *Ibid.*, pp. 83–84.

3. *Ibid.*, p. 84.
4. *Ibid.*, pp. 84–85.
5. *Ibid.*, p. 86.
6. *Ibid.*, p. 90, n4.
7. Krister Stendahl, "Hate, Non-Retaliation, and Love," *Harvard Theological Review* 55 (Oct., 1962): 344.
8. *Ibid.*
9. *Ibid.*, p. 346.

Chapter 21

1. Quoted in Jon Sobrino, "The Historical Jesus and the Christ of Faith: The Tension Between Faith and Religion," *Cross Currents* 27 (Winter, 1977–78): 463, n.27.
2. Minear, *Obedience of Faith*, p. 88.
3. *Ibid.*, p. 89.
4. William Stringfellow, *Conscience and Obedience* (Waco, Texas: Word Books, 1977): 112.
5. *Ibid.*, p. 50.
6. *The Book of Worship for Church and Home* (Nashville: Abingdon Press, 1964, 1965): 38.
7. Arthur B. Ogle, "What Is Left for Caesar?" *Theology Today* 35 (October, 1978): 261.
8. Robinson, p. 137.
9. Ogle, p. 261.

Chapter 22

1. Albert C. Outler, ed., *John Wesley* (New York: Oxford University Press, 1964; "Library of Christian Thought"): 92.
2. *Ibid.*, p. 99.
3. *Ibid.*, p. 92.
4. Minear, *Obedience of Faith*, p. 34, n.4.
5. *Ibid.*, p. 10.
6. *Ibid.*, p. 42.
7. *The Book of Worship*, p. 387.
8. J.C. Hud, "Offering for the Saints," *The Interpreter's Dictionary of the Bible*, 5 vols (Nashville: Abingdon Press, 1976), 5:638.
9. Minear, *Obedience of Faith*, p. 3.
10. *Ibid.*
11. *Ibid.*, p. 4.

Conclusions

1. Max I. Dimont, *Jews, God, and History* (New York: New American Library, 1962): 133.

2. William Sanford Lasor, "An Evangelical and the Interfaith Movement," *Judaism* 27 (Summer, 1978): 336.
3. *Ibid.*, p. 338.
4. Paul J. Kirsch, *We Christians and Jews* (Philadelphia: Fortress Press, 1975): 36–37.
5. Bartsch, p. 336.

Bibliography

Abba, Raymond, "The Origin and Significance of Hebrew Sacrifice," *Biblical Theology Review* 7 (1977): 125ff.

Achtemeier, Paul J., "Mark as Interpreter of the Jesus Tradition," *Interpreter* 32 (October, 1978): 339–352.

Augstein, Rudolf, *Jesus: Son of Man*. New York: Urizen Books, 1977.

Bacchiocchi, Samuele, "Comments," *Biblical Archaeology Review* 5 (January–February, 1979): 9–10.

_____. *From Sabbath to Sunday: A Historical Investigation of the Rise of Sunday Observance in Early Christianity*. Rome: Pontifical Gregorian University Press, 1977.

_____. "How It Came About: From Saturday to Sunday," *Biblical Archaeology Review* 4 (September–October, 1978): 32–40.

Baird, William, "On Reading Romans in the Church Today," *Interpretation* 34 (January, 1980): 45–58.

Barth, Karl, "All," *Interpretation* 14 (1960): 164–169.

Bartsch, Hans-Werner, "The Historical Situation of Romans," *Encounter* 33 (Autumn, 1972): 329–339.

Benoit, Pierre, *Jesus and the Gospel, I*. New York: Seabury Press, 1973.

Berg, Dave, *My Friend God*. New York: New American Library, 1972.

Berkouwer, G.C., *The Triumph of Grace in the Theology of Karl Barth*. Grand Rapids, Mich.: William B. Eerdmans, 1956.

Bokser, Ben Zion, "Religious Witness in Judaism," *Judaism* 26 (Winter, 1977): 63–67.

Bratcher, Robert G., "One Bible in Many Translations," *Interpretation* 32 (April, 1978): 115–129.

Brown, Raymond E., *The Birth of the Messiah*. Garden City, N.Y.: Doubleday, 1977.

Buchanan, George Wesley, *The Consequences of the Covenant*. 20, "Supplements to Novum Testamentum"; Leiden: E.J. Brill, 1970.

_____. "Exploring the Life of Jesus," *The Biblical Archaeology Review* 3 (March, 1977): 33–36, 52.

_____. *Revelation and Redemption: Jewish Documents of Deliverance from the Fall of Jerusalem to the Death of Nahmanides*. Dillsboro, N.C.: Western North Carolina Press, 1978.

179

————. *To the Hebrews*. "The Anchor Bible"; Garden City, N.Y.: Doubleday, 1972.

Buchsel, Friedrich, "Expiation," *Theological Dictionary of the New Testament*. Grand Rapids, Mich.: William B. Eerdmans, 1967: 3:300–318.

Cargas, Harry James, "A Post-Auschwitz Catholic," *The Christian Century* 95 (November 8, 1978): 1063–64.

Charlesworth, James H., "Focus on the Pseudipigrapha," *The Circuit Rider* 2 (September, 1968): 7–8.

Cook, M.J., "Judaism, Hellenistic," *Interpreter's Dictionary of the Bible*. New York: Abingdon Press, 1976: 5:505–509.

Crim, Keith R., "Old Testament Translations and Interpretation," *Interpretation* 32 (April, 1978): 144–157.

Dawe, Donald G., and Carman, John B., editors. *Christian Faith In a Religiously Plural World*. Maryknoll, N.Y.: Orbis Books, 1978.

Dimont, Max I., *Jews, God, and History*. "Signet Books"; New York: The New American Library, Inc., 1962.

Donahue, John R., "Jesus as the Parable of God in the Gospel of Mark," *Interpretation* 32 (October, 1978): 369–386.

Dorff, Elliot N., "God and the Holocaust," *Judaism* 26 (Winter, 1977): 27–34.

Dunn, James D.G., *Unique and Diversity in the New Testament: An Inquiry into the Character of Earliest Christianity*. Philadelphia: The Westminster Press, 1977.

Duquoc, Christian, "New Approaches to Original Sin," *Cross Currents* 28 (Summer, 1978): 189–200.

Echardt, A. Roy, "Christians and Jews: Along a Theological Frontier," *Encounter* 40 (Spring, 1979): 89–127.

Ellis, E. Earle. Review of *Schrift und Tradition bei Paulus: Ihr Bedeutung und Funktion in Romerbrief*, by Hans-Jurgen Van der Minde. *Interpretation* 31 (April, 1977): 204.

Ellison, H.L., *From Babylon to Bethlehem*. Atlanta: John Knox Press, 1979.

Farmer, William, "The Dynamics of Christianity," *Religion in Life* 38 (Winter, 1969): 573–577.

Fisher, Eugene, *Faith Without Prejudice*. New York: Paulist Press, 1977.

Fitzmyer, Joseph A., *Essays on the Semetic Background of the New Testament*. Missoula, Mont.: Scholars' Press, 1974.

Foerster, Werner, *From the Exile to Christ*. Philadelphia: Fortress Press, 1964.

Frankl, Viktor E., *The Unconscious God: Psychotherapy and Theology*. New York: Simon & Schuster, 1975.

Gaster, T.H., "Samaritans," *The Interpreter's Dictionary of the Bible*. New York: Abingdon Press, 1962: 4:190–197.

Godsey, John D., "The Interpretation of Romans in the History of the Christian Faith," *Interpretation* 34 (January, 1980): 3–16.

Grabbe, Lester L., "Orthodoxy in First Century Judaism: What Are the Issues?" *Journal for the Study of Judaism* 8 (1977): 149–153.

Haroutunian, Joseph, and Smith, Louise, eds., *Calvin Commentaries*. "The Library of Christian Classics"; Philadelphia: Westminster Press, 1962.

Harvey, A.E., *Companion to the New Testament*. New York: Oxford University Press, 1970.

Hasel, Gerhard F., "Remnant," *The Interpreter's Dictionary of the Bible*. New York: Abingdon Press, 1976: 5:735–736.

Hellwig, Monica, "Why We Still Can't Talk," *The New Catholic World* (January–February, 1974): 41.

Hendry, George S., "Theological Labels," *Theology Today* 37 (April, 1980): 67–78.

Hill, David, "Paul's 'Second Adam' and Tillich's Christology," *Union Seminary Quarterly Review* 21 (November, 1965): 13–25.

Hoppe, Leslie J., Abstract of "Koncepcja Sadu w Starym Testamencie i w Teologii Pawlowej," by H. Langkammer. *Old Testament Abstracts* 2 (October, 1979): 251.

Hud, J.C., "Offering for the Saints," *The Interpreter's Dictionary of the Bible*. New York: Abingdon Press, 1976: 5:638.

Jepsen, Alfred, "āman," *Theological Dictionary of the Old Testament*. Grand Rapids, Mich.: William B. Eerdmans, 1974: 1:292–323.

Jewett, Robert, "Major Impulses in the Theological Interpretation of Romans Since Barth," *Interpretation* 34 (January, 1980): 17–31.

Kasemann, Ernest, *Perspectives on Paul*. Philadelphia: Fortress Press, 1979.

Kirsch, Paul J., *We Christians and Jews*. Philadelphia: Fortress Press, 1975.

Lace, O. Jessie, *Understanding the New Testament*. New York: Cambridge University Press, 1965.

Lacocque, Andre, *But As For Me: The Question of Election for God's People Today*. Atlanta: John Knox Press, 1979.

Lasor, William Sanford, "An Evangelical and the Interfaith Movement," *Judaism* 27 (Summer, 1978): 335–339.

Legrand, L., "The Good News Bible," *India Theological Studies* 14 (1977): 309–317.

McKenzie, John L., *A Theology of the Old Testament*. Garden City, N.Y.: Doubleday, 1974.

Martin, James P., "The Kerygma of Romans," *Interpretation* 25 (July, 1971): 303–328.

Marxsen, Willi, "Christology in the NT," *The Interpreter's Dictionary of the Bible*. New York: Abingdon Press, 1976: 5:148–149.

Mecklenburger, Ralph D., "Are Christians 'Honorary Jews'?" *The Christian Century* 96 (March 21, 1979): 302–303.

Meyer, Paul W., "The Holy Spirit in the Pauline Letters," *Interpretation* 33 (January, 1979): 3–18.

Meyer, Rudolf, "Circumcision," *Theological Dictionary of the New Testament*. Grand Rapids, Mich.: William B. Eerdmans, 1967: 6:72–84.

Minear, Paul S., *Eyes of Faith*. St. Louis: The Bethany Press, 1964.

_____. *The Obedience of Faith*. "Studies in Biblical Theology" #19; Naperville, Ill.: Alec R. Allenson, 1971.

Moskowitz, Moshe A., "Intermarriage and the Proselyte: A Jewish View," *Judaism* 28 (Fall, 1979): 423–433.

Neusner, Jacob, *First Century Judaism in Crisis*. Nashville: Abingdon Press, 1975.

_____. "Pharisaic Law in the New Testament Times," *Union Seminary Quarterly Review* 26 (Summer, 1971): 331–340.

Nickle, Keith F., "Romans 7:7–25," *Interpretation* 33 (April, 1979): 181–187.

Nolan, Albert, *Jesus Before Christianity.* Maryknoll, N.Y.: Orbis, 1978.

Ogle, Arthur Bud, "What Is Left for Caesar?" *Theology Today* 35 (October, 1978): 254–264.

Outler, Albert C., ed., *John Wesley.* "Library of Christian Thought"; New York: Oxford University Press, 1964.

Perrin, Norman, *The Resurrection According to Matthew, Mark, and Luke.* Philadelphia: Fortress Press, 1977.

Peterson, David L., Review of "Fasting in Israel in Biblical and Post-Biblical Times," by H. Brongers. *Old Testament Abstracts* 2 (February, 1979): 67.

Petuchowski, Jakob J., *Heirs of the Pharisees.* New York: Basic Books, 1970.

Piper, O.A., "Life," *The Interpreter's Dictionary of the Bible.* New York: Abingdon Press, 1976: 3:124–130.

_____. "Suffering and Evil," *Interpreter's Dictionary of the Bible.* New York: Abingdon Press, 1976: 4:450–453.

Porter, Calvin L., "A New Paradigm for Reading Romans: Dialogue Between Christians and Jews," *Encounter* 39 (Summer, 1978): 257–272.

Price, James L., "God's Righteousness Shall Prevail," *Interpretation* 28 (July, 1974): 259–280.

Purvis, J.D., "Samaritans," *The Interpreter's Dictionary of the Bible.* New York: Abingdon, 1976: 5:776–777.

Reimarus, Hermann Samuel, *The Goal of Jesus and His Disciples.* Translated by George Wesley Buchanan. Leiden: E.J. Brill, 1970.

Rivkin, Ellis, *A Hidden Revolution.* Nashville: Abingdon Press, 1978.

_____. "The Meaning of Messiah in Jewish Thought," *Union Seminary Quarterly Review* 26 (Spring, 1971): 383–406.

Robertson, John C. Review of *God as Spirit,* by G.W.H. Lampe. *The Christian Century* 95 (November 8, 1978): 1081–82.

Robinson, John A.T., *Wrestling With Romans.* Philadelphia: The Westminster Press, 1979.

Rubenstein, Richard L., "Response to Tal's 'Jewish Self-Understanding...'," *Union Seminary Quarterly Review* 26 (Summer, 1971): 368–371.

Ruether, Rosemary, "Identities," a review of Marcus Barth's *Jesus the Jew and Israel and the Palestinians. The Christian Century* 96 (March 7, 1979): 254.

_____. Review of *Early Christianity and Society,* by Robert M. Grant. *The Christian Century* 95 (April 26, 1978): 449–450.

Sanders, E.P., *Paul and Palestinian Judaism.* Philadelphia: Fortress Press, 1977.

Sanders, James A., "Torah and Christ," *Interpretation* 29 (October, 1975): 372–390.

Sandmel, Samuel, *The Genius of Paul: A Study in History.* Philadelphia: Fortress Press, 1979.

_____. *Judaism and Christian Beginnings.* New York: Oxford University Press, 1978.

Saunders, Ernest, "Christian Synagogues and Jewish Christianity in Galilee," *Explor* 3 (Winter, 1977): 70–77.

Schechter, Solomon, *Aspects of Rabbinic Theology*. Introduction by Louis Finkelstein. New York: Schocken Books, 1961.

Schillebeeckx, E., *God, the Future of Man*. London, 1969.

Schoeps, H.J., *Paul: The Theology of the Apostle in the Light of Jewish Religious History*. Translated by Harold Knight. Philadelphia: Westminster Press, 1961.

Sheerin, John B., "Has Interfaith a Future?" *Judaism* 27 (Summer, 1978): 308–312.

Sigal, Phillip, "Unfinished Business," *Judaism* 26 (Summer, 1977): 309–321.

Siegal, Seymour, "Discussion: Christianity and Other Faiths," *Union Seminary Quarterly Review* 20 (January, 1965): 180–181.

Sobrino, Jon, *Christology at the Crossroads*. Translated by John Drury. Maryknoll, N.Y.: Orbis Books, 1978.

_____. "The Historical Jesus and the Christ of Faith: The Tension Between Faith and Religion," *Cross Currents* 27 (Winter, 1977–78): 437–63.

Stendahl, Krister, "Hate, Non-Retaliation, and Love," *Harvard Theological Review* 55 (October, 1962): 343–355.

_____. *Paul Among Jews and Christians*. Philadelphia: Fortress Press, 1976.

Stenger, Richard, "Galilee and Christology," *Explor* 3 (Winter, 1977): 57–69.

Stringfellow, William, *Conscience and Obedience*. Waco, Texas: Word Books, 1977.

Taber, Charles R., "Translation as Interpretation," *Interpretation* 32 (April, 1978): 130–143.

Tal, Uriel, "Jewish Self-Understanding and the Land and State of Israel," *Union Seminary Quarterly Review* 26 (Summer, 1971): 351–363.

United Methodist Church, *The Book of Worship for Church and Home*. Nashville: Abingdon Press, 1965.

Vawter, Bruce. Review of "Die wetsgedeettes van die Ou Testament in die prediking," by D.H. Odendaal. *Old Testament Abstracts* 2 (February, 1979): 73.

Via, Dan O., Jr., "A Structuralist Approach to Paul's Old Testament Hermeneutic," *Interpretation* 28 (April, 1974): 201–220.

Wachtel, Nili, "Freedom and Slavery in the Fiction of Isaac Bashevis Singer," *Judaism* 26 (Spring, 1977): 171–186.

Wilcox, Max, "'Upon the Tree'—Deut. 21:22–23 in the New Testament," *Journal of Biblical Literature* 96 (1977): 86ff.

Williams, Daniel D., "Discussion: St. Paul and Tillich," *Union Seminary Quarterly Review* 21 (November, 1965): 27–29.

Williamson, Clark M., "The 'Adversus Judaeos' Tradition in Christian Theology," *Encounter* 39 (Summer, 1978): 273–296.

Williamson, Lamar, Jr., "Translations and Interpretation: New Testament," *Interpretation* 32 (April, 1978): 158–170.

Wilson, R. McL., "Apocalypticism," *The Interpreter's Dictionary of the Bible*. New York: Abingdon Press, 1978: 5:28–34.

Yoder, John Howard, *The Politics of Jesus*. Grand Rapids, Mich.: William B. Eerdmans, 1972.

Scripture Index

Subject Index